Praise for
GET HOME

I0061318

"This book is about so much more than physical self-defense. It's about defenses for the whole self—psychological and emotional defenses to prepare women for a patriarchal world that normalizes violence. This book is much more profound than I expected, and 100 percent the book we need."

—Prisca Dorcas Mojica Rodriguez, author of *Tías and Primas* and *For Brown Girls with Sharp Edges and Tender Hearts*

"In *Get Home Safe*, Rana Abdelhamid offers more than a guide to self-defense; she delivers a heartfelt manifesto for navigating uncertain times with courage, grace, and a deep sense of community. This book is a beautiful offering that equips you with practical tools while also serving as a recipe for resilience in a world defined by uncertainty."

—Silvia Vasquez-Lavado, author of *In the Shadow of the Mountain*

"Rana Abdelhamid weaves together a guide for those who have never experienced violence, those facing it currently, and those coming through the other side. It is a necessary and timely addition to the self-help and feminist canon."

—Mikki Kendall, author of *Hood Feminism*

"With this book, Abdelhamid has given us mujeres a glorious, one-of-a-kind blueprint on how to gather with one another and reclaim the power that is buried in our bodies, hearts, and minds. *Get Home Safe* is activist storytelling at its best: personal narratives grounded in political life with clear guidance on how to transform our day-to-day lives and our communities."

—Daisy Hernández, coeditor of *Colonize This!* and author of *Citizenship*

GET HOME SAFE

A Guide to Self-Defense and Building Our Collective Power

Rana Abdelhamid

ALGONQUIN BOOKS OF CHAPEL HILL

LITTLE, BROWN & COMPANY

Algonquin Books of Chapel Hill / Little, Brown and Company
Hachette Book Group
1290 Avenue of the Americas, New York, NY 10104
algonquinbooks.com

First Edition: February 2026

Algonquin Books of Chapel Hill is an imprint of Little, Brown and Company, a division of Hachette Book Group, Inc. The Algonquin Books name and logo are trademarks of Hachette Book Group, Inc.

The publisher is not responsible for websites (or their content) that are not owned by the publisher.

The Hachette Speakers Bureau provides a wide range of authors for speaking events. To find out more, go to hachettespeakersbureau.com or email hachettespeakers@hbgusa.com.

Little, Brown and Company books may be purchased in bulk for business, educational, or promotional use. For information, please contact your local bookseller or the Hachette Book Group Special Markets Department at special.markets@hbgusa.com.

Illustrations © Areeba Siddique

ISBN 9781643757032
LCCN 2025943328

Printing 1, 2025

LSC-C

Printed in the United States of America

To my parents, Mona and Abdelrazek,
who have forever been my safe space

Contents

GET HOME SAFE

Introduction

Let me know when you get home.

If you're reading this and you're a woman, you've probably said or heard these words. A quiet ritual of mutual survival, a promise we pass between us. These words live in your bones. In whispered warnings. In the careful way you walk home at night.

You think of them again when you hear the echo of footsteps behind you and catch your breath. Do you speed up? Slow down? You grip your keys like a blade, just in case. Maybe you recently bought a container of pepper spray that you carry in a trendy, very small bag, though you don't really know how to use the damn thing. But it's not just walking home alone at night. You worry about your safety and your loved ones' safety in so many situations.

You're afraid to put down your drink in public because what if this is the day someone really does put something in it? Or there's that relationship you can't quite shake, the one that lasted too long, with someone who seemed like a "good" partner until they quietly broke your spirit. You didn't see any red flags, but the whole time they were gaslighting you, manipulating you, abusing you. Maybe you often tolerate blurred lines and gray areas of consent and behavior because you were taught to be "polite" and "kind" before you were taught to set your boundaries and say no. Or maybe you did file the restraining order. You did the "right thing." But that unlocked more anger and now you sleep with the lights on. You travel in groups. Safety in numbers is often the only protection you can count on. Yet, despite all the precautions, the fear remains, because you know that one in three women will experience violence in her lifetime. And sometimes, when you think about the future, another terror strikes you: the fear of what it might mean to raise a child in a world that will inevitably ask them to confront the same dangers you face.

Gendered violence coils around your ankle like a venomous snake, dictating the way you move in all the spaces you occupy. Whether you're walking to class or working late, whether you're praying or dancing or just existing, we know the possibility of gender-based violence is there. Our bodies navigate the world accordingly.

If it feels like you're alone in this, I sincerely want you to know you are not. Almost 53 percent of women in the United States don't feel safe walking home. Not late at night. Not in daylight. Not in their own neighborhoods. Fifty percent of women in the United States feel unsafe simply because they are women. Not because they are weak. But because they live in a world that preys on their strength. And this fear? It's not imagined. It's not paranoia. It's the aftermath of too many real events. Eighty-one percent of women report experiencing sexual harassment or assault in their lifetime. One in three women who've been in a relationship has been hurt by the very person who promised to love them. One in six women in the United States has been a victim of an attempted or completed rape. Around the world, every ten minutes, a woman or girl is *literally* killed by her partner or family member. In fact, in the United States, pregnant women are more likely to be murdered through gendered violence than to die from obstetric causes. Survivors of abuse often get asked: "Well, why don't you just leave?" Yet 75 percent of women murdered by their partners are killed after they leave. Where is safety for women?

Safety is not in our schools. Women ages eighteen to twenty-four who are college students are three times more likely than women in general to experience sexual violence. That age demographic is even more at risk if they're not in school. Safety is not where we work. In the workplace, women are twice as likely as men to experience sexual violence and harassment. Our safety is not online. Thirty-eight percent of women have been abused, stalked, doxed, threatened, all from behind a screen. In our homes, at school, on the street, at work, and even online — where are we safe? Economically, socially, politically, physically, emotionally, women experience violence at unfathomable rates. It is both a slow burn and a sudden blow. Violence lives in the spaces we are told to be grateful for. In the systems that promise to protect us. In the silence that's demanded of us. These aren't just statistics. This is our reality. Our rage. Our resilience. And honestly, sometimes, it makes me want to scream.

We're not apathetic. We do our absolute best to address and confront this violence every day. We are on alert. We create safety for each other in sacred ways, by walking with each other and saying things like "text me when you get home." We wait outside until our friends' doors close behind them. We send live locations before dates, rides, or interviews. Twenty-one percent of us carry pepper spray. We take an Uber we know we can't afford because taking public transport is a risk. We are vigilant, checking the backseat of our cars before we get in, as 61 percent of women globally do. We report violence and we march; we advocate for policy and systemic change. We host healing spaces and remove ourselves from abusive relationships. We speak out, we lead. But then we also know that women who are in the public eye are targets. Almost 90 percent of women in Nepal, India, and Pakistan said violence broke their resolve to be politically engaged. Gendered violence is not just a personal tragedy; it is systemic theft. Of our health. Our futures. Our voices. It is not just an isolated issue. It is a pandemic. You know all this. We know all this. Once you survive, you don't always walk through the world the same way. Those seconds, days, months, and decades after, you exist somewhere in between post-traumatic stress disorder and foggy memory, guilt and shame, anger and sadness, longing and regret. We get up every day and we survive by navigating the world differently. We dress differently. Move differently. We speak with caution, or sometimes not at all. The consequence of gendered violence is scarring in the most intimate parts of you. *Will they even believe me? Was it my fault? Maybe I should have done something different. What if it happens again?* So we bury it. We flinch often and we don't open up. We may never fall in love again. The memory of when we tried to fight still sits in our face and fingers.

Because of gender-based violence we exist with higher incidences of depression, anxiety, eating disorders, and suicide. Because of gendered violence we are less likely to complete our education, secure consistent work, thrive in our careers, and generate wealth. And if you're one of those people who also need economic numbers to care about this, I'll just add that because of gender-based violence, the global economy loses $1.6 trillion annually.

Well, if you're fed up now, regardless of who you are, this book is for you. This book is a little bit about how we got here, but it's mostly about where we can go. How do we keep ourselves safe and keep each other safe when the systems supposedly designed to protect us don't seem to care — if they're not actively conspiring to harm us? The answer is in self-defense.

I'll spoil the ending for you: We *can* keep ourselves safe, and no, you don't have to become a black belt to do it. You don't have to be able to bench a certain amount or be naturally inclined to take on a six-foot-five person on the subway platform. You don't have to be big, tall, or muscular. Self-defense is about so much more than knowing how to throw a punch. It's about healing. It's about organizing. It's about economic justice. It's about the mental and physical well-being that a sense of strength and security brings. It's about confronting the violence that shows up in our homes, our streets, and our workplaces, and building something better in its place.

While the stories I tell here are about the people I have built relationships with, the self-defense tools in this book are presented for everyone. Self-defense can be used by anyone who has been a survivor of violence, regardless of identity. Anyone who has felt afraid for themselves or their friends and family can find tools here to help carve out a safe space for their community in this world.

So how are we still here? How is gender-based violence still this pervasive?

It's almost as if violence toward us is so common that we just kind of live with it. We normalize it against ourselves.

We normalize it against others. I often feel like that meme of a dog saying in the middle of a fire, "Everything's fine," as I handle domestic violence case after domestic violence case, as I teach self-defense class after self-defense class, as I try to pull together an underfunded organization with a very small team, as I read another news story about violence.

Much has been made of feminist progress in this country, but the mainstream feminist movement, particularly in its most visible, institutionalized forms, has too often aligned itself with power rather than challenge it. We are still where we are not because we are failing to resist but because the structures that enable violence are still intact. And too often those structures are being reinforced in the name of progress.

For decades, the dominant and most amplified currents of feminism, shaped largely by the priorities of a small privileged elite, have pursued inclusion into systems of power, corporate leadership, politics, and individual wealth rather than the transformation of those systems themselves. Feminist progress has been measured by milestones like breaking glass ceilings, gaining access to boardrooms, or achieving mere symbolic representation. For example, elite feminism applauds entry into the labor force as empowerment, without acknowledging that poor and working-class people have *always* labored. Often unpaid. Often exploited. Their economic precarity is not empowerment; it is a continuation of violence. But these victories often serve the privileged while doing little to address the structural violence faced by marginalized people worldwide. As bell hooks wrote, "As long as women are using class or race power to dominate other women, feminist sisterhood cannot be fully realized."

When feminism operates in service of capitalism, patriarchy, and the state, it becomes a tool of domination. The figure of the woman CEO is celebrated, even when she leads a healthcare company that profits from medical debt and denial of care. The optics of empowerment mask the reality of extraction. This is not new. From Algeria to Brazil, colonial and imperialist campaigns have long used the rhetoric of "saving women" to justify violence. Feminist narratives are weaponized to prop up war. As recently as the early 2000s, US politicians with no ties to Islam or Afghanistan paraded symbols of Muslim womanhood on the House floor to justify a decades-long occupation that bombed thousands of Afghan women under the guise of "liberating them." As Lila Abu-Lughod writes in *Do Muslim Women Need Saving?*, "The discourse of saving Muslim women from their 'backward' cultures is part of a long history of Western interventions . . . where women's rights were used as a justification for war and domination."

Of course, the United States did not withdraw from Afghanistan because violence against women ended; it simply fell off the state's agenda. We see similar dynamics in

France, often romanticized as a beacon of feminist progress. There is a collective amnesia around the genocide France perpetrated in Algeria, a brutal colonial campaign that killed over one million people, placed two million in concentration camps, and destroyed thousands of villages. French colonialism was justified through the narrative of "modernizing" and "liberating" Algerian women, a paternalistic discourse used to rationalize domination. Today, French state-sponsored secularism still polices Muslim women's bodies, criminalizing hijabs and claiming to "free" women from oppression. This weaponization of feminism also played a central role in the context of anti-Blackness and slavery in the United States. During the nineteenth and early twentieth centuries, white suffragists often promoted narratives that cast Black men as dangerous and hypersexual, using white women's safety as justification for lynching and segregation. Ida B. Wells documented how the trope of the "vulnerable white woman" was repeatedly weaponized to incite racial terror—a pretext for the public torture and murder of Black men and a key tool for maintaining white patriarchal dominance. While white feminists demanded protection and rights, they remained largely silent about this violence and in many cases reinforced it. Enslaved Black women were systematically raped, and after emancipation they continued to be denied protection under the law. For Black women, this meant living in a body that was simultaneously overpoliced and disbelieved.

Their testimonies of sexual violence were ignored in courts, and their labor was exploited in domestic work and share-cropping, without recourse. Mainstream feminist movements rarely fought for the legal protection of Black women from rape or for their inclusion in labor rights organizing, rendering them vulnerable not only to physical violence but also to economic dispossession and legal erasure. Today, these legacies continue in how Black women are often left out of national conversations on gendered violence and in how Black survivors are less likely to be believed, protected, or centered in mainstream feminist movements.

Similarly, Indigenous women were made unsafe by the policies white women "reformers" helped create. The Indian boarding school system, which forcibly removed Indigenous children from their homes, was often designed and supported by white Christian women's organizations. These schools subjected children, especially girls, to physical and sexual abuse, all under the banner of "civilizing" them. White feminists also supported the Dawes Act and other land allotment policies that fractured Indigenous communal lands and disrupted matrilineal governance systems. In the twentieth century, Native women were disproportionately targeted for involuntary sterilizations: Between 1973 and 1976 alone (barely fifty years ago), an estimated 25 to 50 percent of Native women of childbearing age were sterilized without consent by the Indian Health Service, which is run by the federal government and largely employs non-Native doctors. These acts were not only violations of bodily autonomy but also assaults on the continuity of Native nations, carried out in the name of population control, cleanliness, and modernization. Today, Indigenous women continue to face the highest rates of murder and sexual violence of any racial group in the United States, with many cases going unsolved and uninvestigated—a crisis that mainstream feminism has been far too slow to address. White feminism's pursuit of protection, rights, and power often came at the direct expense of Black and Indigenous people's lives, bodies, and families. Rather than challenging white supremacy or settler colonialism, it frequently bolstered both, leaving a legacy of harm that still reverberates through policy, policing, and feminist spaces today.

Feminist movements that center assimilation and symbolic victory while ignoring the structural roots of violence, colonialism, capitalism, patriarchy, and white supremacy leave most of us behind. They tokenize a few while allowing the many to remain unheard and unprotected. They either maintain the status quo or help propagate the extremely brutal realities of state-sanctioned gender oppression. As a result, gender violence persists. Because systems of power remain intact. Because the material conditions that enable abuse, poverty, displacement, war, surveillance, and mass incarceration remain unchallenged.

Indigenous women and women from the global majority (often referred to as the global South) are positioned as victims "needing rescue," and privileged women are tools for patriarchal state and capitalist agendas. Those who comply are rewarded and then often tokenized and weaponized against their own people. Individual success and upward mobility for some (typically those who already had some level of access) are dangled as proof of progress, while the systemic forces, including patriarchy itself, are ignored.

Real change requires a feminism that prioritizes the safety—the emotional, physical, financial, and political safety—of those most impacted by violence. This means listening to and centering the leadership of marginalized people, not as symbols of oppression but as architects of solutions. bell hooks writes, "Feminism in the United States has never emerged from the women who are most victimized by sexist oppression; women who are daily beaten down, mentally, physically, and spiritually, women who are powerless to change their condition in life." Now is the time.

Honestly, after almost two decades of grassroots organizing, I'm over it. I cannot wait any longer. We cannot wait for the institutions that have harmed us to suddenly begin to protect us. We cannot wait for policy to catch up to our pain. We cannot wait for representation to lead to liberation. At a grassroots level, we must build our own safety, physically, through self-defense and community protection. We must heal emotionally, tending to the trauma that violence leaves behind. We must grow our economic power, outside of extractive systems that were never built for us. We must organize politically, not just for access but also for transformation. No one is coming to save us. But we can, and we will, save each other. This is where our safety will grow.

I know this because I am both a survivor of gender-based violence and an advocate against gender violence. It's devastating that when I started this work years ago, I thought the statistics would change. I met and built relationships with thousands of survivors around the world. I listened to their stories and have seen how violence manifests in their lives. I see it every day in my work as a self-defense instructor and as an advocate.

We may feel it in our personal lives. We all see it in the headlines.

I founded Malikah seventeen years ago as an antiviolence self-defense organization dedicated to empowering survivors of violence through training in self-defense, healing, organizing, and financial literacy. At the time, it wasn't an organization; it was just a group of mostly Muslim and immigrant youth learning self-defense and healing together. It was a processing space, a space where I would teach my friends karate, not even with a formal self-defense curriculum. At the time, it was the only way I knew how to heal and process my own experiences of violence. What began as a personal mission has grown into a global movement that addresses safety and builds power with my low-income and working-class communities. Rooted in the foundation of my martial arts training as a black belt in Shotokan karate, the self-defense curriculum that I wrote and which we now teach draws on years of research and the contributions of expert self-defense instructors. I've had the privilege of leading close to eight hundred self-defense classes now, reaching over eleven thousand people across thirty-five countries. This curriculum is now also in use by other coaches whom I have personally trained, mentored, and certified through Malikah. Through these sessions, I have witnessed incredible transformations: people reclaiming their agency, rediscovering their strength, and finding community in spaces built for them to somatically heal and thrive.

My work at Malikah has made it clear to me that safety is multifaceted. It's about physical self-defense, but it's also about economic stability, emotional well-being, and political systems. This understanding has driven us to adapt and expand our programs to address the many dimensions of what it means to feel truly safe and in our power. Since we were founded, Malikah has built loving trust in our community, changed and passed laws, developed an organized membership, and run thousands of programs, all of it a testament to the impact we've made locally and globally.

Through this journey, I've encountered the safety

challenges that communities face, both in my own Muslim-majority immigrant working-class neighborhood of Astoria, Queens, and around the world. These experiences continue to fuel my commitment to ensuring that every individual has the tools and resources to realize their full potential.

Malikah means "queen" in Arabic, but for me, the term also embodies rightful sovereignty, strength, and control, qualities I strive for all of us to embody. Malikah is about more than safety; it's about living with a profound sense of ownership over your body, voice, and life. You are Malikah. You have the strength, control, and authority to shape your own life. Carry that energy with you always.

Malikah has become so much more than a self-defense organization. It is a space where survivors from all walks of life have come together to find support, resources, and joy. Over the years, we've supported those facing domestic violence, helping them find safety and reclaim control over their lives. We've advocated for policy change. We've hosted spaces for celebration, healing, and solidarity. Our work extends to helping women who have just arrived in the United States to tackle food, economic, and housing insecurity through vital programs that ensure women and their families can thrive. In 2023 we opened our first-ever physical space, and we are now expanding to a second and third, creating hubs where low-income and working-class immigrant women can gather, grow, and lead. Through this work I have met so many friends and learned that gendered violence *can* be addressed when we work together, locally.

In every self-defense class I teach, I open with "What brings you to this self-defense class?" I have asked this question hundreds of times and gotten a broader range of answers than you could imagine.

"I was grabbed on the bus on my way home and I haven't felt safe since."

"My husband gets angry easily and often lashes out at me, especially when he's drunk."

"When I was eight years old I was sexually abused by my uncle, and I'm hoping to heal."

"I'm afraid to walk down the street in my hijab because I've been racially attacked before."

"As an immigrant, I need to understand my power and voice in a new country, especially because I don't understand what people are shouting at me."

"I've been kidnapped."

"I want to meet like-minded people."

"There's a bully at school who always seems out to get me. Others say it's because he has a crush on me, but he just makes me feel uncomfortable."

"I was raped on this campus and I'm in class with the abuser."

Every time I have asked this question, regardless of the kind of room I am in or the age group, class, country, or ethnic background represented, there are stories of violence. I have learned through this work that despite the many advancements of our communities and societies that we can be proud of and celebrate, to this day there is no country in the world where women do not experience a disproportionate level of violence.

SO NOW I'LL ask you: Why did you start reading this book?

I can tell you why I'm writing this book: to scale the power of self-defense to more communities and individuals. One woman, after weeks of self-defense training and community support, told me how she finally had the courage to pack her belongings, take her children, and start a new life free from abuse. She went on to join a local support group, where she now helps other survivors find the resources and strength to do the same.

I've seen women use the tools they gained through our financial literacy programs to create entirely new financial futures for themselves and their families. One participant, a single mother who had struggled to make ends meet, shared how the skills she learned at Malikah helped her save enough to start her own small catering business. Through our organizing workshops, I've seen women step into leadership roles within their communities. Through our healing space, another woman, navigating the challenges of single motherhood as an immigrant new to New York City, said she no longer felt alone because Malikah gave her a space to breathe, share, and grow alongside others who truly understood her journey. People often describe the community they co-created here as their "second home." They've decorated our walls with their art, filled our space with dancing and laughter, and transformed it into a safe space where they can bring their whole selves. This is what happens when we are given the tools to not just survive but also thrive and rise to leadership.

I personally have been so transformed through my journey with self-defense. When I started Malikah, I was in dire need of healing and processing my own experiences of violence, and that's what self-defense helped me do. Now we are three generations of women, teaching self-defense with the hope of creating a safer world for women.

My mom, an immigrant who's always had a natural gift for organizing, had never taken a self-defense class before. She was hesitant at first, unsure of what she could bring to the table. Having lived with chronic illness, she was unsure of the power of her own body. But once she started, something clicked. She realized how powerful it was not just to learn physical skills but to feel strong as well. And that feeling of strength was contagious. Now she teaches self-defense in Arabic to women across New York City. She's created spaces where immigrant women can come together, learn how to defend themselves, and feel like they have ownership over their lives. Watching her grow into this role, seeing her confidence and strength shine, has taught me about where my own power comes from. It comes from her.

Then there's my sister. She's a teenager in a New York City public school, navigating all the complexities of growing up in a big city. She's always done karate and has a black belt, but she never imagined she'd be teaching self-defense to other young people. But here she is, working with youth, empowering them to step into their own strength and build resilience. For her, this isn't just about the moves; it's about helping others find their voice and their confidence. It's about creating a space where they can feel seen and strong, especially in a world that often tries to silence them.

Throughout this book, I will make the case that despite the many ways in which experiences of violence try to rob us of our sense of power and security, we still hold power and safety in our bodies. Self-defense teaches that our bodies are our primary site of power: physically, emotionally, economically, and politically. That power starts with (1) healing the self, and it extends to (2) physically protecting our bodies and (3) our material well-being, which enables us to (4) re-create structures and systems through organizing.

Through healing we can collectively confront the systems of violence we internalize and interact with on a regular basis. By fighting back physically, we can regain power over our bodies and deescalate violent situations.

Through economic resilience, we can navigate economically exploitative systems and ensure the material well-being of survivors. Through organizing, we can ask why we are experiencing this violence and how we can collectively learn the skills and organize to create safety concretely for ourselves.

DESPITE HOW GRIM it might sometimes feel, I have woken to marching feet and chanting voices. I have woken to survivors breaking free from years of abuse, reclaiming their power and their bodies, standing tall after storms of violence and fear. I have woken to the strength in our unity as we come together to heal, to resist, and to build a world where no survivor has to endure harm again. We are not just survivors; we are healers, and we are the resistance. This is proof that the power of our bodies cannot be taken away. We hold all that we need to resist these systems.

What if there were a world where we could all come together in healing because we knew where to start? What if there were a world where every one of us knew how to deescalate violence when confronted with it? What if all of our basic material needs were met? What if we all understood ways to organize, to push back, at a community level, against the national and global systems that rob us of our safety? I often ask: What would the world look, sound, smell, and feel like if all of us were safe and all of us were in our power?

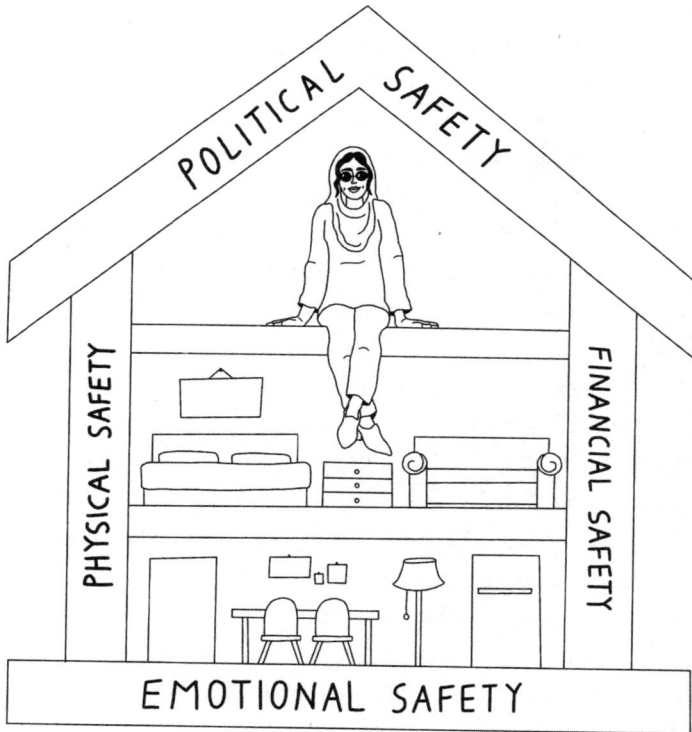

POLITICAL SAFETY

PHYSICAL SAFETY

FINANCIAL SAFETY

EMOTIONAL SAFETY

It's important to answer these questions and envision an alternative reality, so that we can truly see what we are building toward, and as we build, we can find those pockets of safety that already exist in the world as it is. This is why I use the framework of the House of Safety.

For many survivors, home has not always been safe. But this alternative House of Safety serves as a guide. It helps us imagine what true safety could look like and what it might take to get there.

Think of a two-dimensional drawing of a house — you know, a classic kid's drawing, basically a square with a triangle roof on top. This house is built on a foundation of emotional safety. To have a sturdy foundation, we must first address internalized harm and empower survivors to emotionally heal. Without healing the house cannot stand.

Physical safety forms one wall of the house: We lean on the practice of self-defense, bodily autonomy, and freedom from physical violence. Learning to defend ourselves is not just a reaction; it's about reclaiming space and existing in the world knowing that our bodies belong to us.

Next, financial safety forms the opposite wall, providing independence and enabling survivors to leave harmful situations and make decisions that prioritize their well-being. These walls hold the structure upright.

Political safety is the protective roof to ensure that systems, policies, and structures exist to prevent violence. This is why we advocate for policies that ensure that we exist in a world where we don't need to heal from violence, we don't need to fight back against violence, and we don't need to worry about financial insecurity. Political safety shields everything beneath it.

All parts of the house are interdependent and adjoining, just like the realities of violence that our communities endure. Survivors don't experience harm in a vacuum; rather, they experience it in their political, social, cultural, financial, and familial contexts. Consequently, our solutions must also be holistic. Self-defense is one crucial wall, but without the foundation, the opposite wall, and the roof, the house cannot stand.

In the following pages, you'll find tools, stories, and strategies to help you build this House of Safety from the ground up, including:

- Ways to reconnect with your body and begin healing from trauma on your own and in community
- A blueprint for starting healing circles with your people, wherever you are
- Simple, powerful self-defense techniques that anyone can learn, even if you've never thrown a punch
- How to be a bystander who actually makes a difference, and how to deescalate dangerous situations
- Tools for economic safety, from mutual aid to building local economic power
- Strategies for organizing and fighting back against gender-based violence and against the systems that were never built for us
- Real stories of people just like you who are already doing this work and building safety

This book is a love letter, and I say this in the most earnestly poetic, heartfelt, yet non-cheesy way possible. I write this book for my immigrant working-class Egyptian aunties on Steinway Street and my elders in Alexandria, Egypt. They are the women who are unapologetic, bold, proud of who they are, with golden bangles up to their elbows, long flowing abayas, and headwraps. They are farmers who know the soil, the land's rhythms and whispers, as intimately as the verses of the Quran they recite in quiet devotion as the sun creeps back up to light our world. Their heads bow humbly before God, but their spirits rise with a boldness fit for the borough of Queens. They navigate the subway with a quiet power, staring sternly into the eyes of authority without flinching. This book is for them, those whose lives are the foundation upon which I stand.

I write this for the survivors who've sat on the gray couch at the Malikah Safety Center, clutching plastic cups of ice water like lifelines, their voices painting truth across the white bumpy wall in front of them. They are survivors of the violence we're trained to look away from. One owes $30,000 in rent, left by her husband with three kids and no map. One finally walked away after twenty years of violence. One was shoved down subway stairs for wearing her hijab. One is raising two kids alone, working an under-the-table job while fending off a predatory landlord, her asylum claim tied to female genital cutting (FGC), a brutality she never chose. They are not weak. If they wanted to, they could split the earth in two with the force of their love. These women are astrologers of the soul, dream interpreters, survivors, truth-tellers. They are pursued by systems built to erase them, misunderstood by the children they raised with aching backs and quiet sacrifice. Still, they endure. Still, their fingers keep working, kneading dough, braiding hair, sorting rice, reaching for you in the only love language they were ever taught. I write for the women we're conditioned to judge: the ones who get side-eyed for having too many kids, who speak too loud, who "should've known better." The women feminism often forgets.

I write for you if you're sick of this crap—the catcalls, the creepy boss who lingers too long, the man punching women in the face on the subway, the landlord who "accidentally" texts you at midnight. You, who might be holding a little too much, trying to find your footing, hoping for something more. This book is yours too. I write this book because every day I wake up imagining a world where no one has to carry the weight of violence on their shoulders just to get through the damn day.

If you believe in a different kind of world, a world where the weight of oppression does not suffocate your spirit, where the violence of patriarchy no longer binds your hands, and yet you stand, alone in your vision, I write for you. I write for the dreams that live within you.

Your safety, your freedom, your joy—I write for that. I write for all the spaces that you deserve to occupy without fear: school, work, home, public transport. I write for the moments of peace that have been denied to you, the laughter that has been silenced, the love that has been withheld. In every word, I reach for the world that should be ours. A safe world.

This book is your guide toward healing, safety, and power, and I hope it's only the beginning. In the following pages you'll find concrete ways to keep yourself safe and to change the systems that make us unsafe. We'll explore ways to empower our hearts through healing spaces and ensure that we have the economic safety net to have control over our lives.

I hope you take this book and arm your community too. Create your own healing circles. Start or join a self-defense group. Start a financial savings circle. Organize on your block. Advocate for change in your community. Share this with the people in your life, because it's going to take all of us.

I write this book for the same reason I have stepped into rooms across the world to teach self-defense: because every person deserves to live without fear, and because within you lives the power to keep yourself, and your community, safe. Safety is not a privilege; it is the ground on which liberation is built.

Start with Healing

OKAY, SO YOU might be thinking, *Why is this self-defense book starting with a chapter on healing?* It may *seem* counterintuitive to begin with healing before getting to physical self-defense, but the truth is, healing is what allows us to move, to speak, to act with clarity. It's not a detour from self-defense; it's the foundation of it.

First, without healing, safety work can risk reproducing the harms we seek to end. Too often we are taught harmful self-defense practices, based in internalized patriarchal norms, and we can end up reinforcing aspects of the exact culture of violence and victim blaming we're trying to escape. Healing interrupts cycles of violence so that we don't carry them forward.

When I was younger, I spent a summer in Egypt, one of those long, languid seasons when we'd trade the heat of Queens's concrete for the soft breath of the Mediterranean Sea. Time moved differently there: Slow, syrupy afternoons seemed to stretch endlessly toward evening. I remember one dusk, sitting beside my aunt in my grandmother's house, the same home where my mother and her five sisters were raised, their childhood stories tucked into the corners of every room. We were in the living room, where an old, boxy television sat heavy on an equally oversized wooden stand. The red velvet couch beneath us had worn thin over years of bodies resting, stories told, and tea spilled. Its fabric clung to the past like a memory you don't know you're still holding. Golden light poured through the open balcony doors, catching the dust in the air, tiny particles dancing slowly in the fading sun, as if the room itself were exhaling. Then came the *adhan*, the call to *maghrib*, the sunset prayer. My aunt pressed pause on the remote. The television froze. And for a moment the world stilled. We sat in silence, letting the sound of the *adhan* wash over us. The room smelled like her *shai koshari*, strong black tea steeped until almost bitter, then drowned in sugar. The scent wrapped around us, warm and familiar. I listened to the soft, rhythmic crack of sunflower seeds between her fingers — "Syrian seeds," we called them — their shells flicked into a little dish she always kept nearby.

When the TV flickered back on, we were suddenly mid-laugh again. A comedic play, one we'd seen a dozen times before, loud, ridiculous, comforting in its familiarity. We were full of joy, doubled over in that deep kind of belly laughter that leaves you gasping for air, when an ad flashed across the screen, jarring, dark, and unfamiliar. A crying girl. A woman turned away from the camera. A silver blade. A message in stark black letters: "Mother, protect your daughters. This is not from Islam. Don't do it." I remember sitting up straighter, the laughter still stuck in my chest but unable to come out. *What was that?*

I turned to my aunt, confused. "What are they talking about?" I asked.

She didn't answer at first, just sipped her tea and cracked open another sunflower seed. But I was young and persistent, and I kept asking: "What are they talking about?"

Finally she replied. "It's about *khitan*," she said softly. I had never heard this word before. *Khitan*? Like circumcision? My heart dropped. "We all had it," she added, almost offhand. "It's no big deal. It's about cleanliness." I still remember how steady her voice was. How ordinary she made it sound. Something about the way she said it, so calm, so sure, made the pit in my stomach grow even heavier.

"*You* did this?" I asked, my voice small.

She nodded. "It's just what we did. We've done it for thousands of years." She chuckled at my reaction, lovingly amused by how dramatic I seemed. But I was trying to understand how something that felt so deeply painful could be described with such ease.

The TV was still playing, but I couldn't hear it anymore. The joy in the room had vanished. In its place was a silence

I didn't yet know how to name. Then I asked the question I was nearly too scared to voice. Had I had it?

"No," she said. "Fewer people do it now. And you're in Amreeka."

I sat with that for days. Then I buried the memory. I didn't bring it up again. Years later, in college, I chose to write a paper on female genital cutting. I just needed to understand. I started to have more and more conversations with my elders, women's rights activists, my mom. FGC was not some fringe or isolated event. Even with risk of death, severe health complications, and lasting trauma, families forced their daughters to undergo FGC for many reasons, including cultural traditions, religious justification, beliefs about preserving chastity and marriageability, social pressure to conform, and ideas about hygiene and beauty. As of 2021, an estimated 86 percent of Egyptian women between the ages of fifteen and forty-nine had undergone FGC. Today the number is closer to 80 percent, and 37 percent among teenage girls, indicating a sharp decline—because of grassroots organizers, religious leaders, mothers, and advocates.

My aunt was right—FGC *was* thousands of years old and deeply entrenched. But not just in Egypt. There is a long history of genital cutting practices in the Western world as well, though that history is often erased. In fact, in the 1960s an Ohio gynecologist named James Burt performed FGC on at least 170 female patients without their consent. FGC in Egypt is also impacted by Western colonial encounters. British missionaries used FGC as an example of backwardness to justify their ongoing colonial interventions, even while colonial medicine moved the practice into hospitals, legitimizing it and expanding its reach. Even in light of liberation movements, nationalist leaders saw FGC as part of their resistance to Western moralizing and made its defense part of Egyptian identity. Western rule simultaneously condemned, institutionalized, and justified control of women's bodies.

What struck me most was that this wasn't just a story of violence by men against women. It was often other women who performed the procedure. Mothers, aunts, grandmothers, passing it down like a recipe or a prayer. Not out of malice, but out of fear. Out of duty. Out of a belief that this was what made a girl "clean," "pure," worthy of marriage, of protection, of acceptance. This was about survival. And that's what makes it even more heartbreaking. Women taught to carry harm as a form of love. Women taught to cut their daughters to protect them. This was their self-defense.

I don't share this story to judge my aunt. I love her. I understand my ancestors. They were navigating the world with the tools they had, the beliefs they were handed. They made the choices they thought would keep their daughters safe. So much of the violence we face doesn't just come from outside but gets woven into our understandings of love, of protection, of tradition. The only way out is to gently untangle those threads. To mourn what's been done. To name it. And then to imagine something different. Healing doesn't mean erasing that past. It means looking at it with clear eyes and a soft heart. It means asking: What have we inherited? What do we want to carry forward? And what do we want to leave behind?

In fact, healing practice has been one of the most effective tools in the global movement to end female genital cutting. In countries like Egypt, Senegal, and Ethiopia, studies by the UNFPA-UNICEF Joint Programme, an initiative to end FGC, have shown that community-led healing circles, survivor storytelling, and intergenerational dialogue have led to measurable declines in FGC rates. When women are given space to share their stories, grieve what was taken from them, and connect their personal pain to collective action, real change happens.

This is why healing must be at the center of our fight against gender-based violence. Because without it, we are just building new systems on top of the broken bones of the old ones. With healing, we begin to tell a new story. One where love does not hurt. Where tradition makes space for dignity. Where safety begins from the inside out, and then we pass it on.

Often gendered violence reaches our hearts and minds long before it ever touches our bodies. That harm begins early and quietly. It begins in childhood, when children are told to be quiet, to be nice, to not "cause a scene." It begins with school dress codes that simultaneously sexualize and police teenage girls, while we're still told, explicitly and implicitly, "Boys will be boys." It begins when young people are not taught that we are allowed to say no, and when we are not believed.

Gender-based violence gets under our skin because most of us have been taught our whole lives to doubt our worth, to lower our voice, to believe that our value is tied to how small or desirable we can be. It's the same internalized violence that makes us judge someone for not wanting children, or whisper about another who has "too many." It's what makes us question a woman's credibility when we ask "But what was she wearing?" or in the way we say "sorry" all the time. It's why we stay in marriages that suffocate us because we are told that endurance is a virtue and divorce is a shame. We work twice as hard for a fraction of the pay and recognition and wonder if we're good enough. That violence is repackaged as a natural part of capitalism and sold back to us, and we spend billions each year chasing beauty standards that promise us a solution to these ills.

We pass down guilt, shame, and silence generation after generation, through passing judgmental glances and depleted friendships — until we break that cycle. To confront gender-based violence fully, we must unlearn what this world has taught us to believe about ourselves and each other. Healing is not just personal. It is political, ancestral, and deeply necessary.

Healing is so important because violence silences us. When we are harmed, we often feel powerless to name that harm, let alone try to change it. Healing gives us back our voice. Healing reminds us of our boundaries and allows us to move in ways that are authentic. Healing ensures that silence is not our destiny.

When I first started teaching self-defense, I was searching for a place to find and reclaim my own voice after I experienced an act of violence and responded by freezing rather than fighting back with all my might. I remember that in the moment, I felt too viscerally embarrassed to scream or even move. I direly needed a place to process my pain and to feel whole again. I didn't find that at my school or at the local mosque. I didn't have a name for it then, but I needed a space where young women my age could come together to understand our collective experiences and the systems that impose them, and to try to unlearn what we've been taught and come out stronger. A healing justice space is what I began to facilitate as a self-defense instructor.

ONE FALL AFTERNOON, when I had just started teaching, I arrived at a church for a class as part of an immigrant justice program. I pushed through the heavy doors of the building, and a security guard waved me into the auditorium, hardly looking up from her phone. It was in this class that I began to understand healing justice on a much deeper level. The room was small but warm, and there were a few women scattered around. As I started to explain some basic techniques, how to shout "stop" while striking, how to use body weight for effective defense, I felt the energy of the room shifting. There were giggles, some sass, also some intensity. Then a woman named Sara raised her hand. She was quiet, almost hesitant to speak. The interpreter beside her gently encouraged her to share. "I've been thinking about something," she began, her voice soft but clear. "I've been trying to understand why I didn't speak up. It's . . . It's hard for me to talk about." I could tell this was something she was wrestling with. She paused for a long time, taking a breath, as if gathering the courage to continue. I gave her space and the option to not share if she did not feel ready or want to.

But Sara went on, "A few months ago, I was on the bus, and a man—he rubbed himself on me. I didn't say anything. I didn't tell anyone. I just stayed quiet. I didn't want to make a scene. I felt embarrassed. I didn't want anyone to see. I wanted the ground to swallow me whole. I felt like I did something wrong. I didn't want to draw attention to myself. I let it keep happening. And now I can't stop thinking about it. I feel guilt and I feel sadness. I keep asking myself: Why didn't I say something? Why didn't I make it stop?" The room filled with murmurs of understanding and agreement. You could feel the weight of her words settling over us all and the heaviness of everyone's reaction. There was no judgment, just compassion. And in that moment we all started to understand something together: Sara's silence wasn't a choice. It was a consequence of the internalized shame that so many of us carry. The kind of shame that makes us believe that it's somehow our fault. Somehow, whatever our background or culture, we'd all learned that it's better to let the violence happen than to disturb the peace, that there is a shame in speaking up and attracting attention, even when it's to save ourselves. It became clear to all of us that the silence Sara carried was rooted in something much deeper, something she had learned long before that bus ride. I asked her, if she was comfortable, to think about and share a time when she first learned that women were supposed to be ashamed when they experienced sexual violence. She nodded.

"When I was a little girl, my mom told me that I should be careful with my body," she said. "She would always say things like, 'You need to make sure you don't tempt men. Don't be out too late. Don't dress a certain way. If something happens, people will talk. What will they say about you? What will they think of you?'" Her voice wavered as she spoke, and I could see how those words, meant to protect her, had stayed with her, shaping the way she saw herself and how she responded to situations like the one on the bus. The shame was already there, planted deep inside her from a young age. She had learned that if men harmed her, it was her fault. Speaking up would only bring her shame. She was worried she'd be labeled as "too dramatic" or "too sensitive," as though she didn't have the right to be angry or upset, or to speak up for herself. So instead she absorbed the pain, and for so long she let it eat away at her in silence. Those early lessons at home, reinforced by societal messages, subconsciously influenced her reaction to violence. She had stayed quiet not because she didn't have the power to speak up but because she was carrying the belief that somehow it was her fault and that speaking out would only bring more shame. Folks in the room began to chime in with their own similar experience. We all had our own experiences with shame, with silence, with the burden of keeping our voices quiet to avoid judgment. But in that space, we didn't have to carry it alone anymore. It was here that we could begin to unpack it, to heal from it together.

I shared my own experience with the class, trying to connect with Sara and others in the room. I told them about a time in my life when I too had felt a deep sense of shame, a feeling that I couldn't shake off. As a Muslim woman, I'd often felt a weight of expectations and internalized messages: Muslim women are weak, Muslim women are docile. So when I was attacked in the street one day on my way to an internship in Queens, I felt embarrassed to scream and speak up because there was an underlying sense that I didn't want to be seen as a weak Muslim woman. The more I thought about it, the more I realized how these ideas had shaped how I saw myself and how I responded to conflict, to violence. I realized I had internalized gendered Islamophobia the way that Sara had internalized sexism.

"I get it, Sara," I said. "I've been there too. There was a time when I stayed quiet, but I should've spoken up. And it wasn't because I didn't have the power; it was because I had been taught, in subtle and not-so-subtle ways, that my voice didn't matter, that I wasn't supposed to make noise, that I was supposed to endure without complaint."

We talked about the ways society teaches us to be silent, to make ourselves small so we don't upset anyone else. We discussed how the shame we carry doesn't belong to us but is something we've been given, something that has been placed on our shoulders without our consent. We talked about how, in order to heal, we need to unlearn these messages. We need to give ourselves permission to speak up, to scream, to fight for our safety, for our voice, for our bodies. As the class went on, I watched Sara's posture shift. I watched her stand a little taller, her voice growing a little louder when she practiced the techniques. It wasn't just about learning how to strike. It was about finding the power to speak and to not stay quiet anymore.

The third reason that healing is so important is that our bodies remember. Trauma doesn't just live in our minds; it lodges in our muscles and our posture, and it changes how we breathe. If left unhealed, it can keep us from fully accessing the power we hold. To fight back, to scream, and to resist, we first need to release what is holding us down. Healing helps us restore our body to its rightful strength. Only then can our body be our shield and our weapon.

When we learn to fight, we are beginning to heal our bodies from that trauma. Even before this was validated by formal research, so many of us knew it to be true in our bones: that the physical consequences of past violence are not temporary. I have experienced anxiety in the aftermath of violence; I feel it viscerally tight in my gut, buzzing in my fingertips, tense across my face. Growing up in my mosque, I remember elder women creating sacred space in the back corner during prayer times. They would gently place their hands over the parts of your body where you held pain— your chest, your back, your stomach—and in soft, rhythmic tones they would recite verses from the Quran.

Years later, while I was working in a refugee camp in Jordan, a Syrian woman approached me out of nowhere and said I was carrying the evil eye. I had recently fractured my foot and lost someone close to me. I wondered how she could tell I was hurting. For over an hour she laid her hands across my body, from my head to my chest, and recited softly from the Quran. Afterward, I felt lighter. I slept better. My body finally exhaled.

In a maternal health clinic in Mexico, I witnessed another kind of bodywork: a *partera*, or midwife, performing a *limpieza de huevo* for women burdened by emotional and physical heaviness. She would roll an egg gently across the body, absorbing the negative energy, then crack the shell to release what was carried.

In Ghana, I learned from a friend about *kasa*, the practice of speaking openly in community circles to release what is festering in the body and spirit, often accompanied by drumming and dance, allowing the physical body to move grief and fear outward.

In parts of South Asia, especially in Punjabi and Tamil traditions, women perform *jharu* or *nazar utarna*, ritual sweeping or flame-passing, where chili peppers or fire are waved over the body to remove negativity and fear. And in Filipino communities, *hilot*, a traditional form of healing touch therapy, uses massage, herbs, and prayer to realign the body's energies, acknowledging that emotional and physical pains are deeply intertwined.

These aren't just rituals; they are forms of wisdom passed down through generations, each recognizing that trauma is not just in the mind. It settles in the body, in our bones, our skin, our breath. But in community, we can unburden ourselves.

Bessel van der Kolk tells us in *The Body Keeps the Score* that trauma is not just an event that happened to us; it is also the imprint left on our bodies and minds. Van der Kolk is a psychiatrist and expert in trauma. Using decades of research, his book explains that traumatic experiences, especially early childhood trauma, can have lasting impacts on both the mind and body. Trauma literally alters brain function, especially in areas responsible for memory, emotions, and decision-making. Your body "remembers" trauma. It's crucial to understand that healing is tied to bodywork, or somatic healing. Healing, then, must also live in the body, through touch, breath, movement, prayer, and collective care.

One of the most effective ways to confront internalized violence is through consistent, intentional healing practices that reconnect us to our bodies, our stories, and each other. This can include somatic work, like breathwork, body scans, or trauma-informed movement, that helps us notice where we're holding pain and tension. In community, healing can happen through storytelling circles, where we share our experiences without fear of judgment; group meditations or collective prayers that honor grief and joy; artmaking and poetry as outlets for expression; or group walks and nature-based gatherings that restore nervous system regulation. At Malikah, we've found that pairing self-defense with these tools, such as using affirmations before a strike or ending a workshop with collective breathing, helps participants unlearn shame, affirm their agency, and feel seen.

I want to tell you about Lara, a young woman I met through my self-defense work in London a couple of years ago. Lara grew up in London as the daughter of immigrants, in a middle-class home where love was conditional and discipline often came in the form of control and humiliation. From the time she was a child, Lara was told that to be a "good daughter" meant that she needed to be quiet and obedient. Her parents constantly criticized her appearance, compared her to others, and dismissed her emotions. When she cried, they called her dramatic. When she spoke up, she was told she was bringing shame to the family. Her parents didn't hit her, but their words cut deep and shaped her sense of self.

By the time she was in her late teens, Lara entered a relationship with an older man who seemed, at first, to offer the validation she'd always longed for. But that relationship quickly became another site of violence. Her partner isolated her from friends, checked her phone constantly, shamed her for how she dressed, and erupted in rage when she tried to set boundaries. He'd punch the wall next to her face. He'd break things in front of her. He told her she was lucky he "put up with her." Then he would try to win her over with sweet words, apologies, and a rush of kindness. Lara stayed for years, believing what she'd been taught: that her silence was strength, and that love meant endurance. Sound familiar?

Things changed when Lara entered a healing circle we started in London. I remember meeting her for the first time.

She told me after our gathering that she had never heard women speak openly about emotional and psychological abuse before, that she was shocked to hear them name it as violence. Emotional abuse *is* violence. Lara found language for her pain that day. Through collective journaling, breathwork, somatic healing, and storytelling, over the following months, she began to understand how deeply she had internalized shame and fear. She learned to say no, not just verbally but emotionally and spiritually as well. She began practicing self-defense and for the first time felt power in her body, not fear.

WHEN IT WAS time for me to go home to New York, Lara and I stayed in touch. Like for me and so many others, for Lara healing wasn't linear. There were hard days and long periods of grief for the years she lost. But Lara persisted. She left her relationship. She moved out. She applied for a job in youth work, something she had never thought she was "good enough" for. Financially independent, emotionally grounded, and physically empowered, Lara felt fundamentally changed. While as a young girl I never understood the importance of this kind of foundational sense of self-worth, I can see now how my community of women in Queens naturally operated to create this emotional and psychological safety, and how deeply important it was for me when I experienced violence as a young woman.

Let me give you some context. As a child of immigrants, I witnessed my community of women work hard every day to create emotional safety in a world that was not their own. It's a New York City that immigrant women came to and built up, like every generation that came before. Egyptian immigrants like my mama came to New York and settled in Astoria, Queens. At the time, Astoria was not the hip neighborhood of luxury developments and young professionals that it has, unfortunately, become today. My Astoria was always Egyptian, low-income, and working-class. In fact, back in the day, there was nothing luxurious about living in Astoria. Its proximity to the largest public housing unit in North America, to the Rikers Island prison, to underfunded schools, and to the Con Edison plants that gave us the nickname "Asthma Alley" didn't really matter to Mama and Baba and all the Egyptians who flocked there. They were working in Manhattan and couldn't afford city rent, but it's not like they were planning to live there forever anyway. *"Hanirga 'iskinderia el sana el gaya.* We're going back to Alexandria next year." Living in Amreeka was supposed to be temporary, so the cramped one-bedroom apartment for our family of five felt cozier when we were all looking forward to going home anyway.

Despite the challenges, our families, especially the women, created a safe space in Queens. As a child of the diaspora, I can say there is no place in the world that feels more fully home for an Egyptian immigrant than Queens. Because while my elders always romanticized "going back home," they built home right here in Little Egypt. When they realized that we were becoming *too* Queens and less Egyptian, they built Arabic schools and Quran camps. When they saw that Egyptian cab drivers weren't finding halal food to eat during their twenty-hour shifts, they started halal street carts (yes, it was the Egyptians; you're welcome). When my dad wanted to bring home halal meat but couldn't find any, he opened the first halal butcher shop in Astoria. My elders opened masjids (mosques) and Islamic fashion shops; they sold incense, oils, and cassette tapes with Arabic pop songs. Our Eid prayer became an Astoria Park affair, and our Egyptian, Moroccan, and Algerian neighbors' homes became a circuit of childcare. I watched women in my community labor with love for hours to start these institutions; they sold off their ancestral gold jewelry to rent small buildings for schools, and opened their homes to people they had just met. Their hospitality, warmth, and love were why our community was able to survive. They kept us close to them in Queens (sometimes too close, verging on suffocating) because they feared that New York City would shape-shift us to the point that when they looked into our eyes, they wouldn't see Alexandria, Egypt, anymore.

They had no desire to assimilate. They tucked the speaker of their phone into their hijab (think Bluetooth before

Bluetooth) and spoke Egyptian Arabic loudly to their family members scattered across continents, as if they were the only people occupying the sidewalks. They wore their hijabs—bright gold, cheetah print—with long flowy dresses. They brought their Egyptian sounds and flavors and heart everywhere they went, because they loved who they were, despite the racism they faced. They moved like they could see God and God could see them. This community that they built with few resources and lots of vision was the key to their and our sense of safety. Without this collectivist culture, so many of us would have been isolated and struggling more than we already were, emotionally, physically, financially, and politically.

When you know what they were up against, you understand the miracle of what they created. What they were up against was not easy. This was late 1990s and early 2000s New York. This was the height of the global war on terror, when our neighborhoods in New York City were not "cute" or full of cafés with free Wi-Fi. On TV we watched our people and homelands bombed to ashes and metal. On the streets we watched our people in handcuffs get pushed into deportation cells without being given a chance to say goodbye. Informants filled our workplaces and hookah lounges and masjids. There was a never-ending stream of anti-Muslim, and specifically anti-Muslim-women, stories to fill the airways and hearts of the very Americans who chose to sit behind rifles and pull triggers from Baghdad to Brooklyn, all in the name of "safety." But it was a guise for division, hate, and the capitalist extraction of our homelands.

Even amid all this decided lack of safety, Queens felt like the only corner of the world where we could just be. Just be okay.

As a young woman, I found the Queens streets fascinating. I loved how every single neighborhood embodied the ever-growing stories of immigrant uncles and aunties. The crowded bus stops, the smell of halal food carts and incense oils, the hollering of street vendors, and the buzzing of dozens of languages. Languages that all sounded like home even when I mostly didn't understand a single word. Queens is the world. It is my world. To this day, I love and live in these streets, even as their soul fades into the quiet erasure of gentrification and luxury development.

But it was on a Queens block one summer day that I got attacked by a man who tried to take off my hijab. I don't remember much; as is often the case with violence, it all happened so quickly. I was making my way to an internship. I remember I was on the phone, scrambling to dodge people on the sidewalk, running late. Then I remember the force, my head being yanked back, no warning, my feet nearly coming out from under me. My scarf, tightly wrapped around my head so I could show off my signature hoops, was now wrapped around my neck. Suffocating my breath.

I spun around with a gasping force and came face-to-face with a broad-shouldered man, much taller than me, his body hovering entirely over mine. He blocked the July sun that had been beaming on my face just seconds earlier. I felt small, shocked, and afraid. You never forget a look like his. I hope you never have to see one. It was unalloyed hatred. He was looking through me, like the rage was too powerful to focus his eyes. It reminded me of the moments when strangers would mouth "You don't have to wear *this* here" or "Dirty terrorist" at my mama when she first walked with me down these streets, still unfamiliar then, my tiny fingers curled into her sweaty palms. At that moment, and unfortunately in many moments afterward, I felt like I was, quite simply, not human. I struggled, pushed, and was able to duck into a storefront and then into the building where I was headed.

I climbed up the stairs in a complete fog. Luckily the bathroom entrance faced the front door, and I walked right into it. I remember the feeling of my body slumped on the floor of the bathroom, my head between my knees as they shook. I remember choking back loud sobs. More than anything, though, I remember being concerned that someone would *hear* me crying. I felt an immense sense of shame. I must have done something wrong. I deserved this. I felt that my crying would inconvenience the people around me, that I would take too long and someone else would need the restroom. I felt ashamed that this could happen to me. I felt ashamed that

I had let this happen to me. I didn't want anyone to know. Because their knowing what had happened to me would prove the point: *Muslim women are weak. I am oppressed.* For so long, as a young woman I had been fed messages about my body that had become deeply rooted in my heart. It was no wonder my first response to the assault was shame.

When I tell the story of my self-defense journey, I start with this experience. The impetus for starting Malikah was much more complex than one incident. But in that moment, I felt so many things connected. In the years since 9/11, police infiltrated our most private spaces, knocking on the doors of my home, spying on my community members, and sowing mistrust among our families. Every morning, as a public school student, I walked through our underfunded schools, greeted by security guards in the hallways, walkie-talkies squeaking and scratching. And in those hallways, my small, curvy, brown Muslim girl's body was hypersexualized by boys much older than I was. It was normalized that bodies like mine would be groped, touched without consent. *I should want it. It's a compliment.*

It made me hate the ways my body expanded. My body didn't cooperate with clothes. I was made to feel it was unruly. What I saw in the mirror felt painful, so I developed disordered eating habits at age fourteen that shrank my voice and thighs. As an Egyptian woman, I took trips to Alexandria, Egypt, in the summer, where I witnessed other gendered violence. When I was a fifteen-year-old girl, everything around me pushed me to literally hate the body I was in, not to try to understand its power or to protect it. This will feel familiar to you. The layers of various parts of our identities heighten the ways in which we might experience violence against our bodies. In those moments during the attack in Queens that day, and for many months after, I felt that the power of my body had been taken away. I'd lost my power. I felt unsafe in my own skin. I also felt unsafe in my mind.

I was angry at myself, and as the self-hate and powerlessness brewed, I could easily be triggered and flash back to that memory. My parents remember the day it happened. They tell me it was the day that I didn't say one word. Very unlike me. I was too enveloped in my own thoughts. Like Sara, I felt ashamed that I "let" myself be hurt in that way. For a while I didn't share my experience of the hate-based attack with those around me because I was embarrassed and because I didn't want to further blemish the already very blemished narrative around Muslim women. I had to remain strong. I had to be independent. I had to break whatever anyone thought about Muslim women and weakness. When I was prompted to report the incident by those who had been in the office that day, I shook it off. For the five minutes when reporting was even an option, I convinced myself that the violence I had experienced wasn't *that* big a deal; after all, there were no visible signs from the assault on my body marking the incident. Besides, I was a Muslim girl who grew up post-9/11. I knew better than to find safety in the same systems that surveilled my community.

I didn't have the words to describe it at the time, but my experience was a gendered hate crime. After 9/11, hate crimes against Muslims increased by 1,600 percent. And though we don't often think about it, Islamophobic violence is one form of gender-based violence, given the visibility of Muslim women in our hijabs. I write this just weeks after teaching a self-defense class with a group of my Queens elders, one of whom, a hijabi, was pushed down a flight of subway stairs. I remember thinking, *Thank God she only broke her arm*. At another self-defense class I taught one week at a local public high school, a teacher came up to me to tell me that a group of her Egyptian hijab-wearing students were verbally attacked on the bus on their way to school. They felt too afraid to take the bus again. That was why she had reached out to us to come and give a self-defense class. This hate-based violence is ongoing and it's pervasive. It happened to me then and it's happening all these years later.

We all learn to shrink ourselves in response to violence, changing our routes, removing our hijabs, staying silent when we want to speak. I've come to understand that the violence we face isn't random, it's systemic. It's gendered Islamophobia. It's racism. It's the legacy of a post-9/11 world that targets Muslim women for being visible and erases us when we're harmed. The truth is, we are not the problem. And the deeper truth is, we are powerful. But we can't access that power if we're isolated or stuck in shame. That's why healing spaces are so essential. When we gather, when we share our stories and listen to one another, we begin to see the patterns. We begin to unlearn the lies.

JUST LIKE MY elders did when they arrived in a land that met them with violence, I turned to community. As part of my own healing, I gathered with others, the way my elders had gathered before me. What I now call a Malikah Healing Space began as something simple: a few friends and I meeting in a borrowed room in a Brooklyn community center, because no one would give us space in Queens. We were girls from the neighborhood, Muslim, immigrant, daughters of working-class families. We came with wounds we couldn't always name and stories we hadn't yet spoken aloud. So we created our own space.

Every week that first summer, when I was about sixteen, we sat in a circle and talked. It might seem small, or maybe it'll sound radical to you, but to me at the time it felt deeply familiar and deeply necessary. It mirrored what I had watched men do in Egyptian coffee shops, sitting together for hours over backgammon and tea. What my mother did at the mosque with her friends, sharing weeks of life in whispers between prayers.

What that healing space gave me is hard to measure. I didn't walk out magically cured of fear or anxiety. But I did begin to feel rooted. For the first time, I saw myself reflected in others who cared for me, who listened without judgment. That room gave me a sense of control, a sense of pride in my story and my survival.

I began to think of myself as a garden. Before, I had been planted in barren soil that had all its nutrients drained away by racism, sexism, Islamophobia. There was no sun. No water. Sometimes it felt like the world was actively poisoning me, extracting whatever energy I had left. But in that space, with gentle conversation, rituals of care, and truth-telling, I began to grow. To feel fed. My roots deepened. My leaves turned toward the light. I remembered parts of myself I had thought were gone.

WE ALL NEED that kind of space. A charging station. A place to pause, reflect, reconnect, and emerge stronger. As bell hooks reminds us, "Feminism is a movement to end sexism, sexist exploitation, and oppression. . . . [A]ll of us . . . have been socialized from birth on to accept sexist thought and action." These healing spaces do exactly that: They help us unlearn the lies we've been taught about ourselves, the world and build new ways of being.

So I ask you: How many spaces or relationships in your life truly fuel you? Where and with whom are you reminded that you are whole, not broken?

That's why it's not just "healing." It's *healing justice*. Because our pain doesn't exist in a vacuum. We don't do this to excuse violence. We do it to transform it. As Paulo Freire wrote in *Pedagogy of the Oppressed*, liberation begins with critical reflection and collective action. We must recognize that what we're experiencing isn't just personal, it's political. And that understanding this becomes the gateway to safety.

I didn't know that when I was a teenager and walking through Queens in hijab when a man grabbed me and hurled slurs at me, spitting in my face. I didn't know how to name what happened. I just felt ashamed. But in that healing circle, I shared that story and the room didn't flinch. Other women nodded. They had stories too. That space became the first place where I stopped believing the lie that I was alone. We began to name the pattern. And in naming it, we began to break it.

By virtue of who we were, one of the first questions that surfaced in our healing circles was one that had shadowed my self-image for years: Are Muslim women oppressed? Especially in the early 2000s, when headlines, classrooms, and television screens portrayed Muslim women as either helpless victims or symbols of backwardness, I carried the weight of that narrative. It silenced me. It made me feel like I couldn't speak openly about the pain or struggles within our communities without feeding the same Islamophobic stereotypes that already tried to define us. I was constantly living in reaction, responding to how others saw me, rather than living as my full self. I wasn't free. I was navigating the world defensively, shrinking, guarding, translating, explaining. But something shifted as I sat in a circle with other Muslim women, women who carried similar stories in different dialects, different bodies. I began to understand that this narrative of the "oppressed Muslim woman" was never ours to begin with. It wasn't a reflection of our truth; it was a projection. A story constructed by empire, media, war, and racialized patriarchy. A story used to justify invasions and surveillance, to silence us, to flatten us. As Gayatri Chakravorty Spivak reminds us, colonial narratives cast "white men saving brown women from brown men," making healing spaces essential for Muslim women and those harmed by these legacies to reclaim voice, agency, and community on our own terms.

But the truth is that Muslim women are not exceptional in our experiences with violence. We are not uniquely oppressed, nor uniquely free. Like so many women around the world, we navigate harm within our homes, our streets, our systems. But we also carry joy. Resistance. Agency. Complexity.

In our healing space, because of our organic shared experience and shared identities, we began to unpack how this narrative had its roots in colonial history. We felt safe enough to discuss these complexities. We started to read and talk about French colonialism in Algeria. The more we dug into this history, the more I began to see the parallels with our experience in the United States. French colonizers, in their effort to justify their brutal domination of Algeria, painted Algerian society, especially women, as "backward" and "in need of saving." The hijab, a cultural symbol of modesty, was weaponized against us. The French presented themselves as the "benevolent" liberators, coming to "free" Algerian women from the oppressive traditions of their own culture. But as we learned from the work of Frantz Fanon, this wasn't about liberation; it was about control. The French justified their colonial project by claiming that "unveiling women" was an act of salvation, even as it stripped them of their autonomy and resistance. It was a violent attempt to erase an entire culture under the guise of progress. These attitudes didn't die with French empire. They were exported. In the United States, Muslim women became symbols, flattened into caricatures of either oppression or extremism. After 9/11, our bodies were used to tell stories we didn't write, stories that justified war, surveillance, and xenophobia, all under the familiar banner of "saving" us. These narratives are not just historical. They are alive in policy, in media, and even among contemporary French and American feminists who still fail to see Muslim women as full agents of our own liberation.

That history became a mirror for me as I reflected on my

own experience. Why would a random man in Queens feel entitled to impose his will on my body in such a violent way? It dawned on me that this wasn't just about me or my hijab. It was part of a larger narrative that had been imposed on Muslim women for centuries. The violence that had been inflicted upon Algerian women was now being echoed in the way Muslim women were treated all over the West and even in some Muslim-majority countries, like Egypt, where in many spaces hijab is now often seen as "backward" (that is, not Western), associated with lower-class status, and banned. But for me, my hijab was never a symbol of oppression: It was primarily a religious practice, and it happened to also be a reclamation of my identity and my history, one that had been distorted and attacked for centuries.

As we continued to unpack these layers of trauma and history in the healing justice space, I began to feel a shift. I realized that the shame I had carried for so long wasn't mine to bear. It was the weight of a false narrative, one that had been created by colonial powers to justify their violence and control. In the healing space, I found the strength to see my hijab as a symbol of resistance, not victimhood. It was only in this space, surrounded by other Muslim women, that I began to reclaim my power.

After that summer, our group of friends began to ask: How can we bring this kind of collective healing to more survivors of gender-based violence, in more places? Fast-forward seven years, and I was facilitating a multiweek healing space in Boston. We gathered women from across worlds. Each week we sat in a circle, sharing our lived experiences, learning our collective histories, and unlearning the silences we'd inherited. We built trust over stories and shared snacks, over vulnerability and laughter. Week by week, the room became a refuge. One of the women who showed up consistently was Aisha. She often came with her two sons, arriving early and lingering long after the session ended. Her English was clear, but she would still apologize, softening her *b*'s, hardening her *r*'s, like she was trying to fold herself into the space. Urdu was her first language; English was her fifth. She carried herself with warmth and humility. But during the session on gender-based violence, Aisha went silent. Her body tilted slightly toward the ceiling, her eyes glassy, her mouth still. She listened like she was holding her breath. While others shared stories of leaving abusive relationships, she said nothing, but everything about her presence spoke. Her silence was its own language.

It wasn't until several weeks later that Aisha found the words. They came slowly, haltingly, like she was translating pain into language for the first time. She spoke of the abuse she was living through, violence she hadn't named, even to herself. The room stilled. No one interrupted. A few women passed tissues. Afterward, they embraced her. "Thank you," Aisha kept saying over and over, her voice trembling but steady. I remember Aisha not because she laid out a plan for escape but because I watched something internal begin to shift in her. For the first time, she was refusing to normalize the violence done to her. That refusal, that naming, was a turning point. The moment she spoke, she stepped closer to her own freedom.

Years later, after I had returned to Queens, I ran into her by chance. She looked different, lighter. She told me that the women in that healing circle became the women who let her sleep on their couches when she left home. They helped her find a shelter. Her exit wasn't easy. But it was hers. "It was better than the bruises and the sexual violence I endured for years," she said. Aisha didn't find freedom in one moment. She found it in community, in language, in the slow, painful process of telling the truth. That is the power of healing: not just in naming harm but also in building the relationships that make survival, and transformation, possible.

HEALING TO FIGHT BACK

ANYONE CAN START a healing space for themselves and those around them. Just as Alcoholics Anonymous revolutionized peer-led psychosocial support by showing that healing does not require hierarchy or clinical expertise, the healing spaces I run affirm that safety from gendered violence can be both accessible and effective. These are not luxuries. They are community-based, survivor-centered responses to harm, rooted in the kind of care work that for generations has been integral to the health of our communities yet too often dismissed or made invisible.

Research backs what our circles have shown us: that peer support and community-led healing spaces reduce isolation, build resilience, and increase long-term well-being for survivors of gender-based violence. Studies show that trauma-informed group interventions, particularly those centered in cultural humility and lived experience, can significantly improve mental health outcomes, increase feelings of safety and agency, and even lower the risk of future violence. These spaces don't just help us process trauma; they help us prevent it by creating networks of care and accountability.

Healing spaces give us structure and support and permission to be honest. These spaces don't require perfection. They require intention. They can be as simple as a small group that meets once a week in a living room, a café, a classroom after hours, or a community center. You don't need credentials to start one, just clarity, care, and a commitment to safety. What makes a space healing is not the decor or setting but what is held within it: truth, trust, and the permission to be honest.

Start by asking a few people around you, maybe people

who have hinted at wanting more connection, who've shared fragments of their story, who feel safe to you. Ask them: "Would you want to gather regularly to talk, listen, and support one another through what we're carrying?" If you don't know where to start or whom to invite, you can begin with yourself. Use a journal or voice notes. Write your story in fragments. Map your earliest memory of safety, or your first encounter with shame. Or look for organizations in your city centering women's healing and safety. Malikah offers these kinds of spaces, but other organizations exist in cities all over the country. These spaces are not about self-improvement. They are about survival. They are about reclaiming safety in a world that often tries to take it away. And when built with care, they become places where healing becomes possible, not just for individuals but for our entire communities.

Whether you're gathering with friends, colleagues, and neighbors or starting this journey on your own, these principles can guide you in creating a healing justice space that is grounded, intentional, and safe.

A SAFETY HEALING FRAMEWORK

Guided by trauma-informed principles, these six questions are meant to help you reflect on your safety, power, and history to create a shared safe space for your group. You can approach them slowly, address them all at once, or revisit them over time.

1. **What spaces am I a part of, and how do I feel in each of them?** Home, work, school, faith spaces, friendships... Are they safe, neutral, or harmful?

2. **What are my personal safety boundaries? How can I protect them?** Emotionally, physically, digitally... What feels like a no? What support do I need to enforce my boundaries?

3. **What aspects of my story have I not yet acknowledged or processed?** This can include both personal and intergenerational trauma. What pain have I silenced?

4. **What strengths have I developed from my lived experience?** What survival strategies, skills, or wisdom have emerged from my story?

5. **Who are the people I trust to support me and how can I deepen or expand those connections?** Who shows up for me? Who listens without judgment? Who makes me feel safe in my body and voice? What relationships nourish me, and which ones need boundaries or closure?

6. **What kind of world do I want to build around me and what does it look like to feel safe in it?** If safety weren't something I had to fight for, how would I move? Whom would I be surrounded by? What would I create? What would joy look like for me on a daily basis?

You don't need to be an expert to hold this space. You need to be present. To listen. To trust that the wisdom in the room is enough. As a facilitator, your role is to protect the container, not to direct what happens in it. This is shared work. You can use the six questions presented above as guiding questions for each session, one per session. Over eight sessions in total, you can have the first session focus on getting to know the people in the space and setting norms, and the last can be a celebration of your journey together.

At your first gathering, co-create community agreements. Ask:

- ▸ "What do we each need to feel safe and seen here?"
- ▸ "What boundaries should we set to ensure this space stays grounded in care and mutual respect?"

Three key agreements that I've used in my healing spaces are:

1. **Confidentiality.** What is said in the room stays in the room.
2. **Collective care.** We check in with each other and name our needs.
3. **Personal power.** We each take ownership of our story, healing, and growth.

I also suggest that you give the space some rhythm. Predictability helps build transparency and a sense of safety. Maybe you meet once a month for ninety minutes, at the same time, on the same day, and in the same location, and have a consistent opening and closing prompt. You can begin each session with a check-in: "How are you feeling today? One word or pass." "When did you feel a spark of safety this week?" Use guiding questions to anchor conversation: "What story have you carried that no longer serves you?" "When did you first learn about your worth?" You don't need to rush to solutions. Allow moments of silence. Remind people to share as much or as little as they want. The goal is to witness, to process, to start to unlearn false narratives.

What to Do When It Gets Hard

This is trauma work, which means hard things will come up. Emotional triggers, miscommunication, and moments of discomfort are not signs of failure. Offer grounding techniques for everyone. Take a few slow breaths together, feet planted on the ground, looking around the room. Encourage peer support and don't pressure the group to "fix" someone. It's important to remember that a healing space is *not* a crisis intervention center. Healing spaces do not replace professional care. Before you start a group, make a list of crisis hotlines, mental health organizations, and culturally competent organizations. Share it at the start of the space and be clear about what you can and cannot do. You can always offer to connect someone with support beyond the circle you created. It's okay to say, "I care about you and your safety and I want to direct you to support beyond this space." Healing justice spaces must be strong enough to hold complexity, and flexible enough to respond with care.

HOW TO LEAD with trauma-informed care:

1. Pause and ground the room
Take a moment. Gently interrupt if needed and invite the group to pause. You can say: "Let's take a breath together before we continue. I want to make sure we're staying grounded and caring for one another."

2. Return to the group agreements
Revisit the norms the group co-created. Remind everyone of shared values like respect, confidentiality, care, and curiosity. You might say: "Let's return to the agreements we made together. Are we upholding them right now? Is there anything we need to revisit or adjust?" This centers accountability without placing blame.

3. Assess what's happening
If the space feels tense, acknowledge it without judgment. For example: "I'm sensing some tension or hurt right now. That's okay; this is difficult work. We don't need to name it out loud, unless someone wants to. Let's all take a breath together and check in with ourselves. If anyone wants to

pause, know that is an option here." This gives people permission to express themselves without escalating further.

4. Support those most impacted

If someone has been hurt, check in with them quietly during or after the session. Ask what support would be most helpful to them, whether it's time, space, or one-on-one support. Always follow their lead. You might say: "I want to check in with you. Do you need a pause, some space, or something else right now?"

5. Facilitate repair when possible

If conflict arose between group members, invite accountability through reflection. You can ask:

- ▸ "Can we reflect together on what happened?"
- ▸ "What would repair look like for you?"
- ▸ "Is there anything you need to feel heard or safe moving forward?"

These questions encourage ownership, not blame.

6. Follow up after the session

Reach out to those involved to check on their emotional state, clarify any lingering concerns, and reaffirm their belonging in the space. Let them know they are not alone or forgotten. Recommend professional, spiritual, or cultural mental health support when needed. Share the list of mental health practitioners and organizations in the area. Conflict is not the opposite of healing. When held with intention, it can be a doorway to deeper connection, clarity, and care.

A Grounding Practice for Safer Healing

When the energy in the space feels heavy or when you need to come back to yourself, this practice can help. You can guide it aloud for a group or move through it quietly on your own.

1. Set your gaze

Close your eyes or gently fix your gaze on a point in front of you.

2. Embody safety

Visualize a place or moment where you felt completely safe. Breathe into that image.

3. Breathe with intention

- Inhale through your nose: "I am safe."
- Hold for a count of three.
- Exhale through your mouth: "I release what does not serve me."
- Repeat three to five times.

4. Affirm your power

With each breath, repeat:

- ▸ "I am safe."
- ▸ "I am in my power."
- ▸ "I am healing, at my own pace."

5. Return gently

Open your eyes. Check in with your body. Offer yourself gratitude.

Reclaiming Safety, Together

There is something sacred about healing together. I've seen it again and again: How the simple act of gathering, of sitting in a circle, transforms. How a quiet room, filled with held breath and shared truth, becomes a place where shame begins to loosen its grip. That's where something shifts. That's where survivors stop whispering and start reclaiming their voices, not just for themselves but for each other as well. When we do this work together, we remember that we are not broken; we are wise. That our pain is not isolated; it is political, historical, and shared. And that when we speak it aloud, in the presence of others who hold us with care, it begins to lose its power over us. There is deep power in being witnessed. In being believed. In seeing your own story reflected in someone else's eyes. What I've witnessed is this: Women who once shrank into themselves begin to sit taller.

Crying turns into laughter. Strangers become kin. Let me be real: Healing in community is not easy work. But it is holy work. You don't need to be fully healed to start this journey. You just need to be willing to begin, with care, with courage, and with the knowledge that you are not alone.

Celebrating Together

I've learned that one of the most powerful things you can do in a healing justice space is to make time for joy. That's why we celebrate at the end of every eight-week healing circle we facilitate. We close every individual session with something grounding, but the final gathering is intentionally celebratory. We dance, we eat, we share poems and music, and we laugh, sometimes for the first time in weeks. When we've spent weeks unpacking trauma, telling hard truths, and confronting painful histories, our bodies and spirits need space to feel what else is possible. Celebration offers closure. It regulates our nervous systems after intense emotional work and reminds us that we are not just defined by what we've survived. Ending a healing journey with joy helps mark the transition from vulnerability back into the wider world. It grounds us, reconnects us to community, and affirms that healing is not just about pain but also about reclaiming life. Whether you're alone or with others, I encourage you to create a joyful close to this work. You've committed to your own safety and power, and that is worth honoring.

Doing the work to unlearn this internalized harm is life-long. There is no finish line. But the more we reflect, process, and build support systems around us, the stronger we become, not only emotionally but physically, financially, and politically as well. Through my own experience and the experiences of so many marginalized people I've met through Malikah, I've learned that self-protection requires more than just knowing how to fight. Without a sense of emotional grounding and clarity, it's easy to freeze, to doubt yourself, to let fear take the wheel. That doesn't mean you need to be fully healed to defend yourself—none of us are. But healing work helps us reconnect to our power. It builds the self-awareness and critical consciousness that make physical self-defense more than a reaction. It becomes a practice.

That's why the next part of our healing journey focuses on self-defense, not just as a set of techniques but also as a practice of reclaiming your body, your voice, and your right to safety. When paired with emotional healing, self-defense becomes a transformative act of resistance, rooted in power, not just fear.

Defend Yourself

RECENTLY TIKTOK HAS been asking us funny questions. Between a self-defense class and a meeting with our coaches I'll be scrolling, and a hyperenergetic, way too loud video will pop up on my screen for the thirteenth time today: "Bear or Man?" If you've seen the trend, you know what I mean. A loud, chaotic video begins, usually with a woman yelling "Bear or man?," and what follows is a sixty-second breakdown where she explains why, in a specific situation, she would rather face a bear than face a man. Like: "You're lost in the woods. Do you want a bear to find you, or a random man?" And every single time, the answer is a bear. Not because bears are cuddly. A bear might maul you, sure, but it won't gaslight you. A bear won't love-bomb you on Tuesday, isolate you by Friday, and blame you for its claws on Sunday. A bear doesn't send you "u up?" texts after it has harmed you. It just *is* what it is.

Yes, the videos are exaggerated and hilarious, but the fear behind them? That part is so, so real. The reason this trend blew up isn't that women hate men. It's that so many of us are exhausted by the constant calculation it takes to navigate violence, especially when it comes from people we already know. These videos are funny, yes, but they're also a kind of release for the nervous system. A mirror held up to how deeply unsafe we feel, how much we're taught to ignore our gut, and how often our warnings get waved off.

WHAT IS SELF-DEFENSE?

IT MAY SEEM like an obvious question, but self-defense is so often misunderstood. It is not a martial art nor is it a combat sport, although there are elements of my black belt in karate background that were useful to my self-defense journey. For example, learning how to spar, punch, block, and kick—all components of a good combat sport or martial arts work-shop—can be beneficial to elements of self-defense. But not all elements of combat sports and martial arts are beneficial in self-defense contexts.

Self-defense is specifically the act of protecting oneself from harm. Sometimes self-defense is physical, like breaking free from a wrist grab, blocking a punch, or striking to create enough space to escape. Other times it's verbal, like shouting "Back up!" or "I don't know you!" to draw attention and deter an aggressor. Self-defense can also be strategic: moving closer to a group of people on the train when someone is making you uncomfortable, taking a different route home when you are being followed, or scanning a room for exits the moment you walk in. Self-defense can mean choosing not to respond at all. If someone is verbally harassing you on the street and you assess that walking away is the safest option, that *is* self-defense. It's not about pride or proving strength. Self-defense is about staying safe.

Most people are never taught how to face harm. How do you respond to violence or conflict? We are not taught — not in school, not at home, not in the media we consume — what to do. From a young age, we are conditioned in very different ways, depending on who we are. Some of us, especially marginalized people, are taught to endure harm quietly. To be polite when we're uncomfortable. To smile when we're scared. To stay silent to avoid escalation. Others of us, growing up in neighborhoods policed like war zones or in war zones, are taught to fight. To "never let anyone mess with you." To respond to disrespect with aggression, even when that response might put us in more danger, even when walking away would be safer. But rarely, if ever, are we taught the full range of options available to us. We aren't taught to pause, assess, or set boundaries. We aren't taught to deescalate with intention or how to fight back with strategy.

Commonly, we are also taught that violence belongs to the powerful. That abusers, bullies, and those with more money, more weapons, or more status have the right to harm us and get away with it. That calling for help might bring more harm. Violence becomes something done *to* us, something we're supposed to survive, not interrupt. But self-defense changes that story. It says you don't need to be big, fast, or loud to physically protect yourself. You don't need to have power as the world defines it to say no. Self-defense belongs to anyone who has ever been made to feel small, unsafe, or unseen. It's about tools, practice, and strategy. It's about choice. Self-defense is not reserved for the muscular, the able-bodied, the masculine, the fast, or the trained. When I start my classes, I ask, "What does a powerful body look like?" and those are the attributes that most people name. But power is a set of choices and responses that anyone can access, regardless of identity, ability, or experience, when facing harm.

As I've said, self-defense is not always physical and it's certainly not always violent. But sometimes it is. That truth can make people uncomfortable. For most of us, violence doesn't come naturally. In fact, many people internalize the idea that any use of force, even in defense, makes them "just as bad" as the one causing harm. But violence in the context of self-defense is not aggression; it's interruption. It's a last resort, not a first instinct, and there are times when it's necessary.

I've had countless students freeze in class the moment I ask them to raise their voice. Others flinch or giggle when

I tell them to strike. I get it. We've been told all our lives that violence is the problem. That good people walk away, being polite and smiling in the face of anger. That real strength is in staying calm. But what if that isn't always true? When I teach self-defense, part of what I'm asking people to do is unlearn. Unlearn the shame. Unlearn the politeness. Unlearn the lie that says protecting yourself is dangerous. Because here's what I've seen: People walk differently when they know they can fight back. They speak differently when they've practiced saying no like they mean it. They breathe differently when they know that in a difficult situation, even if they froze, even if they walked away, they had options.

Here's the truth that's hard to say out loud: Sometimes surviving violence requires the use of force. But the key difference is that in self-defense you use force only for deescalation and safety. In real life, its application is not black and white. Context matters. If we're not careful, what we think is self-defense can escalate a situation and put us and those around us in more danger. A move that protects you in one moment could escalate danger in another. That's why what's written in these pages is not a one-size-fits-all formula and should never be treated as one. The techniques and strategies shared in these pages are tools that require practice, adaptation, and discernment. Without practice, even the simplest moves may not serve you under stress. When an incident is unfolding fast and your adrenaline is rushing and you're feeling a mix of shock and fear, you're not going to do something you don't feel equipped to do. And no book or class, no matter how detailed, can predict the exact circumstances you may face, nor guarantee your safety. Each situation is unpredictable, and only you can assess what feels possible and effective for the exact moment you're in. There is no way to play out every single scenario in advance.

This guide is meant to prepare you with the options that can expand your awareness, sharpen your instinct, and build your confidence. I will offer strategies to draw from, but none of them are intended to replace your judgment. My hope is that through this you'll be able to build the confidence and self-trust to choose when and how best to apply these techniques, to mitigate risk, to address violence, and to move toward safety for yourself and your community.

I don't teach self-defense because I believe fists can fix the world. I teach it because we all deserve every possible tool to survive, and to thrive. Sometimes the most radical thing someone can say is no, and sometimes they have to say it with their voice, their hands, and their feet. This isn't about teaching you how to walk away quietly. It's about teaching you how to fight when you need to, because you are worth protecting. Your life, your dignity, your safety — they matter. And if the world won't give you safety, then you have every right to take it. Yes, I want you to be a fighter. Not someone who seeks violence, but someone who will meet it with fire when it comes. Someone who knows how to defend their life like it's sacred. And once you know that, once you feel that truth in your bones, no one can ever take it from you.

Denormalizing Violence

Every day, we're bombarded with stories of violence — in the news, from our friends, in our communities. None of these stories is an isolated tragedy; all are part of a devastating pattern. A pattern of silence, complicity, and systems that continue to fail us. We are told to wait for justice, for policy, for change, while enduring violence with no tools to navigate it. Self-defense is not a solution to gender-based violence. It will not dismantle patriarchy, end femicide, or fix what centuries of injustice have broken. It should never be the only line of defense, nor should it be the burden that survivors must carry alone. But self-defense *is* one form of resistance, and to learn it is to break the silence and challenge the normalization of violence by refusing to accept its inevitability. It is not just physical skills but also about self-worth, boundaries, and collective protection.

I just read a headline. It says that a woman who was a finalist in the Miss Switzerland competition is dead. As I read closely, I learn that she did not die of some natural cause. I learn that she was murdered by her husband. Her name is Kristina Joksimovic and when she died her body was chopped into small pieces with a jigsaw. This was after he strangled her, but before he put the bits of her body into a blender. Kristina Joksimovic, a mother and finalist in the Miss Switzerland contest, is now a puree and the news is saying her husband has a confirmed mental illness.

I just read a headline. It says a woman who is an Olympic medalist is dead. She did not die of some natural cause. Her name was Rebecca Cheptegei. Her organs failed her. But this was only after the world had failed her. Her boyfriend glazed her body with gasoline and then lit a flaming match to kiss her skin. Three-quarters of her body was eaten whole by fire. One-quarter was left as a reminder of who she once was. The media says she died by fire in Kenya.

Another headline. A woman in France is seventy-two and has been married for fifty years. Three people call her mom and seven call her grandma. For ten years she slept in the bed of a man who would drug her and then invite other men to rape her. For ten years she slept while her neighbors raped her. Gisèle Pelicot had to look into the eyes of fifty-one of her rapists in a court of law. Her husband drugged her and invited seventy-two men into her home to rape her. The media asked if she was a swinger.

I just read a face. She's sitting, pale and gray, on a gray couch in front of a bright wall that reads MALIKAH SAFETY CENTER. I want to tell her there is no safety here in this world for bodies like ours as she lifts her face veil to tell me her story. I am distracted by the crookedness of her nose, where his fist struck her face over and over again. I am distracted by the bruise under her lip, where his fingers pressed into her face over and over again. But somehow I am hearing every word she says just as she pulls out her phone to show me battered images of her legs. *"Shayfa?"* she asks me in Egyptian Arabic. "Do you see?" Her eyes search for belief in mine. My fingers cover hers as I gently nudge away her phone. *I believe you. You don't have to show me anything.* She is quiet now.

She has sat on this couch before, lingering to tell me stories, seemingly disconnected ones — about a time in a park, or about her son's dating life: *"Tiftikiri agawizo?* Do you think I should get him married?" — maybe without knowing exactly why she is sharing them. But she and I have both always known why she is here on the gray couch. This is the first time she has told me the whole story.

"I believe you," I say.

"Darabny, wi mish awal mara, bas ana khalas," she tells me. "He hit me, and not for the first time, but I'm done."

Each time she visits I learn more about her. Usually she is funny. She makes our whole office laugh. Sometimes she just stops by to bring us food she's made. Today she is not funny. Today her spleen is ruptured, and she was up all night in the emergency room. Yet the media will never know her.

WHENEVER I TEACH a self-defense class, and as I sit writing this chapter, I feel conflicted. Because the truth is, I know that the burden should not fall on us to have to learn to protect ourselves. The real solution is so much bigger than learning to fight back in the moment, than us taking that burden on ourselves. I often tell my students, "My dream is to never teach another self-defense class again, because that would mean there's no violence left for us to defend against."

But I think about it this way: If someone is coming to you hungry because they have not eaten in two weeks, you won't go off about the climate change, capitalism, and corruption that leave so many people in the world hungry. The first thing you do is give them something to eat, and then you might go work to change the systems that have left them hungry in the first place.

In my self-defense classes, I go off about the root of the issue, believe me. I also see self-defense as a means of creating a new culture, the culture we *want*. A culture of safety, where we are healed and where we understand the power of our bodies. We need to shift our relationship with violence and stand against any form of its normalization.

Self-defense classes, if taught properly, do this. Self-defense classes can be revolutionary, like any education space. We can't pretend the violence isn't happening. It's happening against us now and it will keep happening for a while longer. As much as I wish this were not true and as much as I organize and build the movement so that maybe one day this will not be true, for now it is true. We can sit in that powerlessness, or we can learn how to defend ourselves. As a survivor of violence, I became a self-defense instructor when I finally accepted this fact.

Most people who know me think my journey with self-defense started after I experienced a hate-based attack, but really my need for safety started much earlier than that. My journey with karate started when I was seven. Every Sunday my brother and I made our way down along Ditmars Boulevard, past brightly painted graffiti, Tony's Bike Shop, and MTA tunnels, to a mosque in Queens called Dar al Dawah. I would wear my white gi and slip on a pink one-piece hijab, excited to step into the mosque basement, which doubled as a karate dojo (a remnant of Black Muslim organizing in NYC). Usually I was one of just a few girls in my karate class. I noticed that. This was at least in part because many of the parents in our community did not want their daughters to train under a male instructor. As we got older, more and more of my girlfriends were pulled out of the class.

But I stayed in the class because I was bullied in public school. The first time I was shoved into a wall, hands around my neck and all, was in kindergarten. I was a small-framed, brown, hijabless, but clearly Muslim girl with glasses, a love of books, and no chill for playground politics. In other words, I was prime bullying material. So my parents signed me up for karate.

At first it was about survival. But soon it became so much more. It gave me something the world kept trying to strip away: confidence in my voice, power in my body, and the kind of discipline that no one could shove out of me ever again. And when I really think about it, my parents enrolling me in that mosque-based, mixed-gender Shotokan karate class was less about extracurriculars and more about resistance. In our Queens neighborhood, a lot of parents tried to protect their daughters by keeping them away from certain spaces, especially ones with boys or uncles. But my parents? They went the "prepare her for battle" route. My dad was like, "I can't be there every time, so you better know how to handle yourself." (True story: When I left for college, he made me watch *Taken* with him and said, deadpan: "Just so we're clear, I'm not Liam Neeson.") My mom, meanwhile, was the original fighter. She never backed down for anyone, not a landlord, not a racist, not even her own family, and she made sure I knew: "Your body is yours, and you protect it like your life depends on it. Because sometimes it does."

So from the ages of seven to fifteen, I trained relentlessly, sparring, memorizing kata, traveling to compete across the city and even the country. By the time I passed my black belt exam, I could hold my own in the ring. But back then, I didn't connect it to safety. I didn't yet understand that every punch, every kick, every shout of "Kiai!" was laying a foundation not just for competition but also for survival. I loved the ritual of it: bowing and saying "respect" before stepping onto the mat, honoring the space we shared.

As I was growing up in New York City, physical displays of toughness were everywhere. It was in the way people held themselves on the subway, bodies tense, ready. In the way you walked down the street, fast, firm, eyes forward, no room for hesitation. It was in the way some kids at school bumped shoulders in crowded hallways, some postured, and some just stayed alert. Being able to assert yourself physically wasn't just for defense; it was how you got where you were going in a crowded city that was constantly in motion. It was how you claimed space, stayed aware, survived. And inside that dojo, I was learning how to move through the world with my head high, my body grounded, and the knowledge that I could protect myself, not just from strangers but also from the idea that I had to make myself small to stay safe.

It wasn't until after I experienced a hate-based attack that I truly began to take my self-defense education seriously. Being physically assaulted in public shattered something in me. It shook my sense of safety in the world and in my own body. For the first time, I wasn't just learning to defend myself as a skill or a hobby; I needed it as a lifeline. In the aftermath, I threw myself into training: I took self-defense workshops, studied Muay Thai and boxing, and deepened my commitment to karate. But more than anything, I began to yearn for a space where I could explore and reclaim my physical power. I found myself daydreaming about what it would mean to pass these tools on, to help others feel what I was starting to feel again: strong, grounded, capable. Teaching my first self-defense class didn't just help me feel safer walking down the street. It transformed my relationship with my body. For the first time since the attack, I wasn't afraid of being seen. I wasn't shrinking. I was standing tall, and I wanted others to stand with me.

Self-Defense Is for Everyone

I'll never forget the workshop we held one summer evening in Astoria Park, right by the East River, where a New York City bridge cuts across the sky like a spine of steel. The sun was starting to set, casting gold over the grass, and the breeze off the water made the heat bearable. We had carved out a quiet corner near the running track for our class, surrounded by the sounds of kids on scooters, uncles arguing over cards, and a neighborhood moving through its evening rhythm. That day we were focused on a basic wrist grab escape, a simple technique that could make the difference between danger and safety. Strollers were parked at the edge of our circle. Friends held each other's bags while they practiced.

I noticed one woman, Mariam, standing off to the side.

She had stayed quiet during the warm-up and now looked like she wanted to disappear. Her arms were crossed tightly over her chest, her body completely still. I walked over and asked gently if she was okay. She paused, then whispered, "This just happened to me."

She told me that two weeks earlier, a man had followed her home from the grocery store. He grabbed her wrist and tried to drag her toward the street. She didn't scream. She didn't run. She froze. "I thought I wasn't going to make it home," she said. Her body now was remembering something she didn't want to remember. She was freezing again. And still she stayed for the rest of the class. She watched as others learned how to break the grab, how to turn their hips, how to drop their weight. Eventually, quietly, Mariam stepped forward. "Okay," she said. "I'll try."

She held out her wrist, and we practiced together. One repetition. Then another. With each attempt, her movements became clearer, more confident. By the fifth or sixth time, she wasn't just trying; she was doing. The next time someone tries to take her power from her, she'll have a response, not just a reaction. In a world that too often takes and takes from us, that is power! That is the power of training. Of being ready. Of remembering that you are not helpless, even if the world has tried to make you feel that way. That's why I teach self-defense. Because I've met too many people like Mariam, people who freeze not out of weakness but because no one ever taught them what else to do. Because we've been taught to be polite instead of prepared. To avoid being "too much." To hope, in moments of danger, that staying still might be enough.

Let's be clear: *Hoping* is not a strategy. Power is. Preparation is. Practice is.

So if you're reading this wondering whether self-defense is for you, whether you're strong enough, loud enough, brave enough, the answer is yes. This book is your class. Your space to learn. Your invitation to fight, not for violence's sake, but for your safety, your dignity, and your right to move freely in the world.

THE PRINCIPLES OF SELF-DEFENSE

SELF-DEFENSE ISN'T JUST about throwing a strong strike (though don't get me wrong, we *will* get to that). It's about knowing how to show up in your body with clarity, power, and care. At its core, self-defense is about deescalation: of violence, of fear, of the narratives that tell us we aren't allowed to fight for ourselves. These principles are here to remind you that the most important part of any self-defense practice isn't force; it's preparation, presence, and practice. It's how we teach our bodies to say "No," "Not today," and "I'm in charge now" with or without words.

Here's how I start each of my workshops:

Principle	Summary
1. Reject Victim Blaming	We don't learn self-defense because the violence we experience is our fault; we learn it because we deserve to survive. Whether you froze, yelled, walked away, or fought back, you did what you had to do. This isn't about blame. It's about options. And the violence you experience is never your fault.
2. Heal Through Your Body	Your body remembers. So, we move. We kick, block, breathe, and stand tall, not just to fight but to heal as well. Every move says: *I'm strong.*
3. Consent, Always	Before every technique, we ask: "Can I try this with you?" That's the rule, every single time. Because practicing self-defense *starts* with respecting each other's boundaries. Period.
4. Practice Builds Power	Freezing is normal. But with practice, your body learns new moves. Self-defense becomes muscle memory, something you can call on when you need it, without even thinking twice.

Over the years, I've had women call me after an incident, shaken, breathless, adrenaline still pumping, to say, "Rana, it worked." And my first response is always heartbreak: "I'm so sorry this happened to you. Are you okay?" But my second feeling? It's gratitude. That she had the tools. That she remembered her power. That she got to get away.

That's what happened with Mariam. She didn't just come to class; she came back to herself. She turned fear into action. And that choice, that moment of *I'll try*, changed everything. My hope is that the pages ahead serve as a guide for you and for anyone you love. May these tools help you walk through the world just a little taller. May they remind you that you are not helpless. You are powerful. You are worthy of safety. And maybe, just maybe, this book will be the start of your self-defense journey too. Just like it was for Mariam.

Stay Sharp

I TEACH YOUNG people, and I teach elders. I teach trainers, and I teach first-timers. I teach law professionals who wear suits, and I teach street vendors who just got off a shift. I teach in Arabic; I teach in Spanish; sometimes I teach with interpretation. I still teach in masjid basements. But I also teach in parks, community centers, conference rooms, and now, finally, in our very own Malikah Safety Center in Queens.

At every class, I learn from the people around me. I've sat with women who've escaped armed kidnappings. Competitive fighters. Students. Parents. Survivors who are just starting to reclaim space in their own bodies. I ask them about their first experiences with self-defense — whether it was a class or an instance in which they unfortunately had to use it.

There's always a range of stories, experiences, and entry points. And the truth? A lot of people's first experience with self-defense ... well, it isn't great.

Maybe you've taken a self-defense class before. Maybe your first class was led by someone who didn't look like you, who didn't understand where you were coming from and didn't really care to. Maybe it was a guy with cop energy (or actually a former cop?), cracking awkward jokes between drills. Maybe he called you "sweetheart" and "honey" and it made your skin crawl. *Eye roll.* Maybe there was no space to talk about how it *felt* to imagine being attacked. No moment to pause, reflect, or reconnect with your own sense of power. Then when you left, you were half triggered, half confused, and not sure what you got out of it. That's why I created something different.

At my classes, we open in a circle. We set boundaries. We laugh. We name our fears out loud. We practice using our voices, even when they shake. And when we move, we do it in ways that feel accessible, whether you're wearing jeans and sneakers or a jilbab, whether you're postpartum, disabled, or simply tired. No expectations. We talk about real situations: walking home from work, dealing with harassment on the train, being followed while wearing hijab, experiencing harm from someone you love. We ground everything in consent and choice. You can sit out. You can take a breath. You can cry. You can say no. That is self-defense too.

We make space for culture, for language, for the sacred. I've had aunties break into *du'a* (prayer) in the middle of class. We've shared stories in Arabic, Spanish, Urdu, Wolof, and Bangla. By the end of the class, people are walking out not just with techniques but also with a self-defense mindset. Because before it ever gets physical, self-defense is mental.

You need to feel safe to develop that self-defense mentality: trusting what you notice, internally and externally.

WHAT IS SITUATIONAL AWARENESS?

SITUATIONAL AWARENESS IS key to self-defense. Before we ever learn how to strike, we learn how to notice. It begins with awareness. It begins with what you feel, in your body, in a room, on a street corner. And it starts in two places: within yourself and in your surroundings. First, you learn to build and trust your self-awareness, the internal alarm that tells you when something doesn't feel right, even if you can't explain it yet. Then you strengthen your ability to observe what's happening around you: energy shifts, body language, exits, red flags. These observations, both internal and external, make up your situational awareness.

Self-Awareness Is Safety

Many of us are taught to quiet our inner safety voice. The voice in our gut. The one that tightens when someone stands too close. That whispers, *Something is off.* So we smile instead of act. We're polite instead of firm, to make others comfortable, even when we feel uncomfortable.

Take a second right now and listen to your safety voice. Tune back into your body's alarm system that we were taught to ignore. Self-awareness is our internal compass, and like any compass, it gets clouded, whether by trauma, as a result of gaslighting, or from years of brushing things off. But it can also be recalibrated. You can retrain yourself to trust what you feel.

There is a moment that I will never forget, from a virtual self-defense class I taught for 850 women in collaboration with a national organization, in which we discussed the importance of self-awareness and trusting your gut. The second I said the words "trust your gut," people on the call started to chime in about all the times they had discounted their intuition. One woman wrote in the chat about her daily commute, how a stranger on the train would stare at her intently every morning. He always stood a little too close, even when the train was empty. One day he followed her off the train, trailing her from a few feet behind. She felt it immediately; her shoulders tightened, her breath quickened. But she told herself she was overreacting. She didn't want to seem rude or dramatic. It wasn't until he turned down the same side street she did, a street he had no reason to go down, that she began to sprint. She reached a nearby bodega, heart pounding. She waited there in the bright light for a while and eventually made it home safe, but the real fear came after: *What if I hadn't listened to myself then either?*

Another woman shared a story from college. One afternoon she headed to a study group in the dorm room of a guy she barely knew. The second she stepped inside, her gut reacted. The lights were low. The door clicked shut and locked behind her. No one else had shown up yet, even though the group text had said four o'clock sharp. She noticed how he stood between her and the door. How he kept offering her something to drink, brushing off her questions about where everyone else was. Every part of her body was telling her to leave. But she stayed, afraid of seeming rude, of overreacting. "I didn't want to make it awkward," she wrote in the chat. She left ten minutes later only when someone else arrived unexpectedly and she then found a socially acceptable excuse to exit.

In his book *The Gift of Fear*, Gavin de Becker makes an argument in support of fear by telling us about Kelly. Kelly was on her way to her house with grocery bags that she could barely carry. A man appeared and offered to help her. Despite struggling, she at first politely thanked him and told him she did not need him. He became more and more insistent and charming, even saying, "You don't look like you got it.... I'm going to the fourth floor too.... There's such a thing as being *too* proud, you know." For what felt like a long time she didn't let go of the bags, but eventually she did. Once he did her a favor, Kelly felt indebted to this man she had just met, felt obliged to be kind to him. Even though she was terrified, her need to be polite overcame that. "Hey, we can leave the door open just like the ladies do in old movies. I'll just put the stuff down and go. I promise." She let him in, but he did not go, refused to leave, and insisted that she sit down. She was terrified but still tried to rationalize her fear.

It's so heartbreaking to write this. Kelly was raped for three hours, gun to her head. In her own apartment. Just after she went to buy groceries.

But let me be clear: This story is not here to teach us that there are rapists lurking around every corner trying to help us with groceries. It's not about planting fear; it's about planting *trust*. It's about trusting your gut. Because Kelly *knew*. She felt it. She saw red flags everywhere: his insistence, his manipulation, the way he pushed her boundaries. But like so many of us, she'd been trained to override those instincts. Trained to accommodate and to be "nice." This story is heartbreaking not just because of what happened but also because it shows how far we are taught to bend ourselves to avoid discomfort, even when we're in danger. Trusting your gut isn't about being paranoid. It's about being free. Free to name what doesn't feel right. Free to act on it. Free to choose yourself, even if it means seeming "rude." From a young age, this freedom is taken from us. We are often socialized to suppress our emotions and intuition, even in situations where we may clearly be in danger. We're taught to avoid conflict, to prioritize being liked, and to steer clear of behaviors that might be seen as too assertive.

Carol Gilligan, a prominent American psychologist, found that as we grow older, our ability to listen to our own instincts and express dissent often decreases because of social pressure to preserve relationships and avoid disapproval. She writes that societal expectations often push women to priortize relational harmony and the feelings of others over their own needs. The pressure to maintain peace can silence our inner voice, even when it's urging us to take action. In her work on moral development, she shows how from as early as childhood we are taught to value care and connection over individual voice, which can lead to a disconnection from one's own needs and intuition. Think about how often we're told, "Be nice. He's only teasing you because he likes you," or "Don't be rude," when someone invades our personal space or makes an inappropriate comment.

So we learn to smile, laugh it off, or stay quiet. Over time, that behavior becomes automatic, even when the stakes are higher.

Research on emotional labor, like the work of sociologist Arlie Hochschild, shows that women are expected to manage not only their own emotions but also the emotional experiences of others, especially in public or professional settings. This regulation is demanded even in moments of fear or distress. Emotions like fear or discomfort are framed not as signals to be listened to but as inconveniences to be concealed. These deeply rooted gendered expectations position us as caregivers and peacekeepers. We are consistently dismissed, even in medical environments (like I was when I was giving birth and was given an epidural incorrectly three times even after I let the nurses know). Studies show that women's pain is often underestimated by doctors, and women are more likely to be told their symptoms are "psychological" or stress-related. This affects our physical health, but it also teaches us not to trust ourselves. When you're repeatedly told that your body is not the best judge of what's wrong, you start to doubt your signals. This is how self-awareness gets numbed. Sometimes this is just kind of messed up and annoying. Other times it literally puts our lives at risk.

It is self-defense for us to unlearn these patterns of emotional regulation and regain trust in ourselves. Reclaiming and trusting our intuition is not just empowering. It gives us the ability to make decisions for our safety with clarity. It helps us recognize and respond to danger more effectively. What's fascinating is that the science backs this up. So much research shows that we're actually very good at reading vibes. Studies in neuroscience have found that women, on average, have more active mirror neuron systems, the parts of the brain involved in empathy and emotional recognition, which makes us more attuned to subtle emotional and nonverbal cues than men. Other studies have consistently shown that women outperform men in decoding body language and facial expressions. We pick up on tone shifts, energy changes, the microsignals in a room. We're taught that our emotions are unreliable, that our fear is irrational, that we're overreacting. That's what's unnatural. The very thing we're really good at—intuit, sense, read between the lines—is the thing we're told to mute.

As an Egyptian woman, I grew up surrounded by a deep respect for this kind of self-awareness. My grandmother's intuition was a road map for our family's safety. Her dreams, the way her heart would pound, how her eyes would flicker, or how her palms itched—these were all signs we listened to. This wasn't superstition; it was tradition, and it kept us safe. It was common knowledge that my grandmother's gut feelings could tell us when to cancel a trip, when to call a loved one, or when something bad was about to happen. Like the time she told my aunt not to get on a particular train, which ended up crashing. That story was passed down for decades, retold with flair and drama over a steaming glass of mint leaves and red tea. Meanwhile, I'm out here in Queens, New York, barely remembering my dreams because I go to sleep worrying about the chaos in the world and wake up already bracing for more. Maybe I'd understand more about the world and my place in it if I just listened. Listened to my body, my heart, my energy, my dreams. My intuition. The truth is that our culture tells us that intuition is soft. But it's not. It's data for our safety. It's survival. And it's time we start honoring it like the strength it is.

As you're reading this, maybe you're thinking about those red flags you dismissed or all those times you disregarded your own boundaries because you didn't want to create a fuss or be disagreeable. Who taught you that being liked is more important than being safe? Who taught you not to trust yourself?

Or some of you might be reading this thinking, *I'm the opposite.* You've seen too much. Lived through too much. You don't ignore red flags. In fact, you see them everywhere. You've built walls so high, it's hard to let anyone in. If that's where you are, understand those instincts too. Think about where they come from, and when and how they serve you or don't. Situational awareness isn't about living in a constant state of fear or isolation. It's about clarity. It's about being able to assess real-time information, your gut, your surroundings, your context, and make grounded choices from a place of power, not panic. True self-defense doesn't mean distrusting *everyone.* It means trusting your ability to discern, to navigate risk without letting fear make every decision for you. You deserve both safety and connection.

HOW DO WE BUILD SELF-AWARENESS?

IF YOU WANT to build a stronger self-awareness, you have to treat it like a habit. Intuition sharpens with daily practice. Start by paying attention to how your body reacts in different situations. Throughout the day, check in with yourself: *Are my shoulders tight? Is my breathing shallow? Do I suddenly feel drained or on edge?* These are signs. Instead of brushing them off, start tracking them. At the end of each day, jot down one or two moments where your body gave you a signal, even if you didn't act on it. You can keep this in a journal, a note on your phone, or even in your calendar. Over time, you'll start to notice patterns in how your body responds to certain people, environments, or situations. In the morning, ask yourself: *What do I feel in my body right now? What do I need to feel more grounded today?* At night, reflect: *When did I feel off today? Did I ignore any of my feelings? Was there a moment I wish I had made a different choice?* Keep your answers short and honest. Try not to overthink it; it's about getting used to tuning in to your body.

You can also begin to act on small instincts in your everyday life. If you feel like leaving a space, leave. If someone gives you a weird feeling, take a step back. Don't wait for a major safety situation to start trusting yourself. Build that trust in the low-stakes moments. The more you respond to your gut, the clearer and more reliable it becomes. At the same time, try to create even five minutes of quiet each day, no phone, no scrolling, no input. That space is where your instincts get louder. Finally, watch how you talk to yourself and how others talk to you. If you catch yourself saying "I'm probably overreacting" or someone else telling you "You're just being sensitive," pause. Reframe it: *My feelings are valid.* That simple shift is part of the work. That's how self-awareness grows, not all at once, but moment by moment.

One tool that I like to teach for reconnecting with your intuition is called T.U.N.E. In. (I love a good acronym.) It's

T.U.N.E. In

Take three deep breaths.

T: Temperature + Tension

Notice your physical state. Are you hot, flushed, cold, or sweating? Where is there tension: shoulders, jaw, chest, stomach?

U: Urges

What is your body urging you to do right now? Do you feel the urge to leave, speak up, stay quiet, shut down, freeze? Honor the signal before rationalizing it away.

N: Nervous System Signals

Is your heart racing? Are your hands shaking? Is your breath shallow? These are real, valid cues that your nervous system is picking something up, even if your mind hasn't made sense of it yet.

E: Environment

Scan your surroundings. What are your senses telling you? What do you hear, smell, feel, see, or taste? Is anything suddenly too loud, too close, too quiet, or just off in some way? Pay attention to shifts, as they often reflect internal cues. (We're about to talk about this more.)

a quick check-in that helps you pause and assess how your body is reacting before your brain talks you out of it. The truth is, our bodies often know before our minds do. Your heart might start racing before you fully understand why. Your palms might sweat before you can name the discomfort. If you've spent years being told to ignore those signals, this tool helps you build the habit of listening again.

External Awareness Is Safety

If self-awareness is about recognizing what's happening inside of you, external awareness is about recognizing what's happening *around* you. The two work hand in hand. You can't respond to a situation if you don't know how you're feeling, and you can't respond effectively if you're not paying attention to what's unfolding in your environment. Self-awareness keeps you grounded. External awareness keeps you ready. Are you ready?

In the context of gender-based violence, this kind of awareness is crucial. So many of us are taught to keep our heads down. To walk fast, not make eye contact, stay quiet. But shrinking is not safety! It's conditioning. Real safety comes from being able to read a situation, know where the exits are, sense when something shifts in the energy of a room, and act early. Just like self-awareness, this isn't about fear or paranoia. It's about being alert and being prepared. It's about expanding your field of vision so that you're not caught off guard. External awareness includes noticing who's in the room, who's watching, who keeps showing up in your spaces. It means keeping track of exits, obstacles, who's around you, who's too close. It's reading body language, tone, space, and patterns.

The same forces that diminish our sense of self-awareness also teach us to override what we notice, to dismiss red flags, to normalize discomfort, and to stay in unsafe situations longer than we should.

Then there's the impact of technology — or, as I like to call it, the reason half of us would walk right over a cliff if Google Maps told us to. We spend so much time looking down, deep in our group chats, headphones in, fully dissociating on Instagram, that we've become completely disconnected from what's happening around us. We are missing the world! Research backs it up: A study found that people who use their phones while walking are significantly less aware of obstacles, people, and potential threats. You know, just minor details like that.

Imagine not noticing a whole person doing something potentially harmful to you right next to you because you're busy trying to redownload Snapchat for the twentieth time. That kind of disconnection makes us vulnerable. We miss cues. Like with self-awareness, external awareness doesn't mean living in fear; it just means looking up sometimes. Putting your phone away when you're walking home. Scanning the room when you enter a space. Rebuilding the habit of *noticing*. Because you can't respond to what you don't see, and Siri is seriously, for real, not going to save you.

Relying on your senses when you can for situational awareness helps you become more effective in responding to abrupt changes in your environment or abnormalities. Once you perceive, you can begin to comprehend. What does what you observe tell you about how you and the people around you might be impacted? Let's take a quick journey on my daily commute home in New York City. It's late at night — because when am I ever not working late? — and I'm waiting for the train. The platform's mostly empty, just a few people spread out along the edges. Down the way, I hear a group of three people talking loudly. At first I tune it out, but then their voices shift; they are shouting now, and it sounds like there might be a fight. Here's how I would lean into my external awareness. Because I'm paying attention to my surroundings, I don't have headphones in and I'm focused on where I am; I perceive what's going on. The raised voices grab my attention, and when I glance over, their body language adds an additional perception: tense shoulders, shoving, aggressive hand movements, and a lot of pointing. This isn't just loud talk; it's clearly an argument spiraling into something more. Next, I comprehend the situation. It's late, the platform's nearly deserted, and this confrontation could escalate fast. No workers are around, and no one else is close by to help if things go sideways. This isn't the kind of place where I want to chill and wait for a train. So then I reflect on what might happen. This could escalate quickly, especially if someone's carrying a weapon or looking to provoke further. I think ahead: If this turns physical, where am I? Too close? Trapped? Alone? I take a breath, and I try to act with clarity. I decide to move. I take a few steps back, away from the group, and position myself closer to the stairs. It's well lit there, and I'm near an exit if I need to leave quickly. I don't stare — no need to escalate by drawing attention to myself — but I keep them in my peripheral vision.

In my classes, I ask people to pause and look around them. What color are the walls? Where are the windows? Where are the exits in the space we are in? Are there items around them that could be used as weapons? Shields? Are there people we can go to for support if needed? In a world of short attention spans and social media, I don't think you would be surprised that Dr. Gloria Mark, a psychologist and Chancellor's Professor of Informatics at the University of California, Irvine, who has been studying attention spans, has found that our attention spans have been shrinking over the past two decades. When she started measuring attention spans in 2004, the average was two and a half minutes; in 2012, it was seventy-five seconds; and in the past five years it was forty-seven seconds. We are really struggling to pay attention out here. It's no wonder awareness can be so challenging. Having control over your attention span in a society that is constantly vying for sixty to ninety seconds of our mind space is powerful, if you think about it.

Finally, external awareness isn't just about identifying threats; it's also about recognizing sources of safety. It's not only defensive; it's proactive. Safety isn't just about escaping; it's also about knowing where you can land.

Sharpening your external awareness takes practice. It won't feel natural at first, especially if you've spent years being told to keep your head down or stay in your lane. But like anything, it gets easier the more you do it. Start by building a habit: Every time you enter a new space, whether it's a store, a train, a meeting, or a party, pause for just five seconds before diving in. Look around.

Who's here?

Where are the doors?

What's the energy in the room?

Are people relaxed or tense? Is the space crowded or open?

How do I feel here?

Do I know where I would go if I needed to leave quickly?

Next, begin to identify places and people that feel familiar or grounding. Do you walk the same block every day? When you move through the world with your eyes open, you start to map out not just what feels off but also what feels good. Do you pass the same bodega every morning where the worker always nods at you? That could be a place to duck into if you feel like you're being followed. Is there a crossing guard, an elder who sits outside on your block, or a street vendor who shows up at the same time every day? These people can become part of your safety network, familiar faces who ground you and make you feel safe. You can also ground them, if they ever need it.

SITUATIONAL AWARENESS 101

SITUATIONAL AWARENESS IS what happens when self-awareness and external awareness work together. It means being in tune with what's happening inside your body *and* paying attention to what's going on around you. One of the tools I teach to build this skill is the safety zones framework: green, yellow, and red. These zones combine awareness of yourself and your surroundings to help you figure out where you're at in each moment and what kind of action might be needed. This is typically a good framework to employ before springing into action.

When I introduce this in my classes, people sometimes think these zones have to do with distance from a potential threat—that one zone means you're closer to danger than the next. But the reality is, your intuition can be riled up by online violence or by a brief, passing encounter. They're about how you feel in each moment, physically, emotionally, and energetically, and how your body is responding to what's happening around you. These zones represent different levels of perceptions of safety, specific to a given situation, and understanding them is an effective tool to monitor potential for violence. What zone are you in, and what needs to happen next for you to get to safety?

The green zone is when you feel calm, grounded, and fully present. Your body is relaxed, your intuition isn't raising any alarms, and you're in a state where you can be open, whether to conversation, to connection, or to just enjoying your space. I remember standing at a bus stop in Queens after teaching a self-defense class. It was late, but I felt totally at ease because I was with a friend. I had clarity, control, and confidence. For many of us, these moments when we feel completely safe and not on edge are rare. Recognizing when you're in the green zone is important, because it reminds you of what safety *actually feels like* in your body.

The yellow zone is when something shifts. Your internal and external cues are tingling. You don't feel unsafe, but you're paying closer attention. Maybe someone's body language is off. Maybe the energy in the space changes. You're not panicking, but your senses are more alert. This is the zone many of us know too well: walking faster at night, changing train cars, or pretending to talk on the phone because something just feels *off*. At the bus stop that night, when someone stepped closer than necessary — not threatening, but just a little too much — I shifted into yellow. I started scanning my surroundings, rechecking my exits, preparing my next move. This is a critical zone. It's where you gather more information and give yourself permission to act early, not later.

The red zone is when your body is telling you: *This is not okay.* You feel tense, activated, maybe even afraid. Your intuition is loud now, your heart's racing, your jaw's tight, your thoughts speed up. This is where you need to respond. Someone's following you. Someone touches you without consent. Someone says something that crosses a boundary. At that same bus stop, the moment a man asked where I was going and pushed for my number, my body was locked up. That was the red zone. I knew I needed to create distance, assert boundaries, and get safe. In these moments, you don't second-guess yourself. You act.

These zones give you a map, a way to label your experience and decide how to move. They're about getting ahead of the moment. So, in summary:

Green Safety Zone: Safe

What it feels like:

- You're calm, grounded, relaxed.
- Your heart rate is steady.
- You feel in control and present.

Examples:

- You're at home with trusted loved ones.
- You're in a familiar neighborhood during the day.
- You're talking with a trusted friend.

What to do in this zone:

- ▸ **Regulate.** Seek out habits and rituals that regulate your nervous system (breathwork, journaling, prayer, movement).
- ▸ **Reflect.** Plan for future risks from a place of peace.
- ▸ **Reinforce.** Strengthen relationships and routines that reinforce this safety.

Key reflection: *I feel safe. I am open and comfortable.*

Yellow Safety Zone: Caution

What it feels like:

- ▸ You're uneasy, alert; something might be off.
- ▸ Your heart rate is slightly elevated.
- ▸ Your gut instincts start whispering.

Examples:

- ▸ Someone is seemingly walking behind you.
- ▸ You're in an unfamiliar place at night.
- ▸ A conversation turns uncomfortable or invasive.

What to do in this zone:

- ▸ **Assess.** Scan your environment. What's the source of discomfort?
- ▸ **Set boundaries.** Create space or assert yourself.
- ▸ **Prepare to act.** Mentally map exits, identify allies, ready your voice or body.

Key reflection: *Something feels off. I need to pay attention and decide what to do.*

Red Safety Zone: Immediate Danger

What it feels like:
- ▸ You're panicked, fearful, triggered.
- ▸ Your body is flooded with adrenaline.
- ▸ Your senses are heightened, thinking may narrow.

Examples:
- ▸ Someone grabs you.
- ▸ You're being followed and cornered.
- ▸ A verbal altercation escalates into violence.

What to do in this zone:
- ▸ **Act.** Use verbal commands, self-defense skills, or escape.
- ▸ **Seek safety.** When the moment passes, find safety and support, and regulate your nervous system back to the green zone.

Key reflection: *I am not safe. I need to act quickly to protect myself.*

> #### ✔ Hot Tip: Check Your Bias
>
> Check your bias when assessing what safety zone you're in. Ask yourself: *Am I uncomfortable because of how*

someone looks, their race, gender expression, age, class, or clothing? Or am I uncomfortable because of how they're behaving toward me? There's a big difference. This isn't about scanning for people who "look suspicious." It's about noticing what people are doing. Are they following you, invading your space, staring, escalating contact, ignoring your boundaries? That's behavior. That's a red flag. But just feeling uneasy because someone looks different from you is not a threat; that's bias. And if you don't learn the difference, you're not sharpening your instincts but, often, are reinforcing stereotypes and perpetuating violence. Safety work demands more from us. If we want to be safe and just, we must build real discernment. That means tuning in to your body and your surroundings and being honest about the assumptions you bring into a space. Because your gut can pick up on danger, but it can also pick up on fear that was taught to you. You must ask: Is this fear mine? Is it earned? Or was it planted in me by a world that criminalizes certain bodies? That's the self-defense mindset.

How do you get better at checking your biases? Start by tracking your first impressions. When you feel discomfort, name what it's tied to. Is it the person's behavior? Or something they represent to you? Diversify your spaces, your media, your conversations. Notice who you assume is "safe" and who you assume is "unsafe" and ask yourself why. Talk to people who challenge your worldview. Slow down your judgment long enough to gather actual information. Bias thrives in split-second assumptions. It's lazy and it's life-threatening. Awareness—real, disciplined awareness—takes a little more time.

BOUNDARY-SETTING IS SAFETY

ONCE YOU'RE ABLE to start identifying your green, yellow, and red zones, you are better equipped to understand your boundaries. Building situational awareness (external awareness + self-awareness) requires getting clear on your boundaries and being willing to hold them. The reality is that many of us have never taken the time to define what those boundaries are. What are you okay with? What are you not okay with? What kind of physical touch, emotional energy, or tone makes you feel safe and what doesn't? A boundary is a limit you set to protect your body, your heart, your time, and your energy. Your boundaries can shift and that is natural. Have you ever sat down and named those limits for yourself while in a green zone, when you're grounded and clearheaded? Or are your boundaries mostly shaped by what others have told you is acceptable, what's "not a big deal," what's "normal," what you should "just get over"?

We often end up trying to figure it out in real time, in the middle of a weird hug, a passive-aggressive comment, or a conversation that suddenly went from chill to why-is-my-soul-leaving-my-body, and that is not a great time to reflect.

Boundary-setting might feel like something to do in therapy, but it doesn't have to be anything formal or jargony. For you, it might sound like:

- ▸ "I'm not comfortable with that."
- ▸ "Don't touch me."
- ▸ "I need some time to rest before I can respond."
- ▸ "That topic is off-limits for me."
- ▸ "No, nope, nah."

But when your boundaries are blurred and not defined, it becomes harder to know when they've been crossed or when you might need to say something from the above list. That's when people hesitate in the yellow zone. That's when red zone moments get rationalized instead of addressed. You might think, *Maybe I'm overreacting.* (Or someone might say to you, "You're overreacting.") *Maybe it wasn't that bad.* Saying no might feel rude. Asking someone to step back might feel extra.

Start by asking yourself: *What does respect look like to me? What does disrespect feel like in my body? When do I feel taken advantage of, spoken over, touched without consent, or made to feel small?* These are the starting points for identifying boundaries. Write them down. Make them real. Be specific: *I don't want to be touched without asking. I don't want to talk about my body at work. I need people to stop interrupting me in meetings. I'm not okay with someone trying to change my no into a yes.*

For example, say someone at your job makes a "joke" about your appearance, and instead of setting a boundary, you laugh it off. You don't want to seem uptight in front of your coworkers. But inside, you feel uncomfortable and disrespected. That's a blurred boundary.

Another: You're on a date, and someone keeps pushing your physical limits, not in a clearly aggressive way, but in a persistent one. You start negotiating with yourself. *I guess I didn't say no forcefully enough. Maybe I led them on, gave them reason to think I was into it.*

That's what it looks like when boundaries haven't been clearly defined in advance, when we're trying to figure them out in real time instead of having already named what's okay and what's not. Let me be clear: This isn't about blaming anyone for freezing, second-guessing, or going along to stay safe. That's survival. This is about giving ourselves the tools to feel more confident and prepared before those moments happen, to the extent that we can.

And, of course, it's okay if a boundary becomes clear to you in the moment. Sometimes we don't know something is a boundary until it's been crossed. You're allowed to act on that realization. You can say no, stop, or shift course, even if you hadn't thought about that boundary before or if you change your mind. The point isn't to have everything figured out; it's to stay connected enough to yourself that when something doesn't feel right, you can respond. The more you practice naming and asserting your boundaries in everyday moments, not just in emergencies, the easier it becomes to feel that internal shift when something crosses your line. That's what gives your awareness precision. You don't have to guess whether something's wrong; you *know*, because you've already decided what right looks like for you.

Boundary work and situational awareness are inseparable. They're the groundwork for safety, for clarity, and for choice.

Once you know your boundary, enforcing that boundary with others is self-defense. No one, and I mean no one, should have access to your body, spirit, time, or energy without your explicit consent. You know what's a real turn-on? Consent. You know what's real sexy? Respect. You may have heard the acronym F.R.I.E.S., coined by Planned Parenthood, which defines consent as freely given, reversible, informed, enthusiastic, and specific. While it's often talked about in the context of sexual boundaries, consent applies everywhere. You don't owe a stranger a smile. You don't have to let someone walk you to your door. You don't have to accept help with your groceries if it doesn't feel right. You don't need to justify your boundaries, and you don't need to feel bad for saying no. If someone responds to your no with pushback, charm, or pressure, that's not a misunderstanding. That's your red zone. Gavin de Becker, in *The Gift of Fear*, identifies behaviors like unsolicited promises, excessive charm, and ignoring boundaries as signs that someone may be trying to override your agency. When you notice those patterns, don't talk yourself out of what you feel. As I like to say, *please* let "denial" *only* be a river in Egypt.

To make this even easier to remember, here's another acronym created by university scholars and students.

C.L.E.A.R. About Consent

Choice-based: You have options. This isn't forced.

Lived: You feel safe in your body with the decision, not detached or frozen.

Evolving: You can change your mind at any point.

Active: Silence, pressure, and confusion are not consent.

Respected: If someone won't take your no, they don't deserve your yes.

The more grounded you are in your own awareness, the easier it becomes to communicate what you want and what you don't. Learning self-defense builds that confidence. It helps you trust what your body is telling you, respond when something feels off, and take up space without apology. As you think about your boundaries and learn self-defense, you will build your physical and mental resilience to more effectively establish your boundaries. It's like strengthening a muscle: The more you practice, the more capable you become of standing firm in what you need and want for your own well-being. Each time you say no without flinching, each time you walk away without guilt, you are practicing real safety. That's what a self-defense mindset looks like: one boundary, one choice, one clear no at a time.

FIGHT, FLIGHT, FREEZE... FAWN AND FLOP

WHILE I'VE SPENT the last few pages talking about trusting your gut, let's be real: Our instincts aren't always strategic. Shocking, I know. Our bodies are wired for survival, not nuance. So when a situation escalates, we tend to do one of five things: fight, flight, freeze, fawn, or flop. These are legit nervous system responses biologically wired to protect you, not character flaws. Sometimes they keep us safe. And sometimes... they don't. That's why part of this work is learning not only how we *can* respond but also how to respond in ways that are strategic, grounded, and safe, not just automatic.

I can't stress enough that these are natural responses. I

don't want you to feel bad about what comes naturally to you, but I do want you to be aware of it, and to begin to operate from a place of discernment and not automation. Fight, flight, freeze, fawn, or flop? That's just me when I see my frenemy, my landlord, and my former boss...all in one subway ride. I've usually experienced all five nervous system reactions before the train even hits Ditmars Boulevard on a random Monday. That's why part of building a self-defense mindset is learning to recognize those patterns and unlearning the ones that don't serve us.

Training Your Instincts

When we're under threat, our bodies respond fast, often faster than our minds can catch up. These responses are natural and rooted in both our biology and our lived experiences. Most of us have heard of fight, flight, and freeze, the classic stress reactions that kick in when your nervous system perceives danger. Your heart races, your vision narrows, and your body wants to either run, fight back, or completely shut down. What many people don't realize is that there are two other common responses: fawn and flop. These reactions are just as real, just as powerful, and just as misunderstood. All five are part of what experts call the autonomic nervous system's survival response.

I'm someone who tends to jump straight into fight mode. I pop off fast. Someone says something about Queens not being the best borough, adrenaline kicks in, and suddenly I'm ready to go. But that's not always helpful, obviously. For example, sometimes fight mode can escalate a situation when what I needed to do was to pause, assess, or walk away. Each mode can be helpful or unhelpful, depending on the situation.

Reaction One: Fight Mode

Fight is when your body directly confronts a perceived threat, either physically or verbally. Your adrenaline spikes, your muscles tense, and you feel ready to do something to stop the harm. This response demands that you assert yourself. It's your body's way of saying, *I will not be controlled.* For many people, especially those who've been harmed before, fight mode can feel like the only way to respond. And sometimes it works. But the key is knowing when this response will keep you safe and when it might put you in more danger because it could easily escalate a situation unnecessarily.

✕ Ineffective Fight Response

Fatima was at a party when someone made a degrading comment toward her in front of others. She felt cornered, humiliated, and disrespected. Her body jumped straight into fight mode. Without thinking, she shouted at the perpetrator and swung at him. But instead of backing down, he got angrier. He pushed her hard, and the situation escalated from a verbal one to a physical one. A bystander had to step in to break it up, widening the impact of the violence to others. Fatima's instinct to defend herself was valid, but her automated response didn't give her space to assess whether the moment called for physical confrontation. Because she reacted automatically instead of strategically, the violence got worse for her and people around her.

✔ Effective Fight Response

Leila was walking home late at night when she noticed a man following her. She crossed the street. He did too. She slowed down; so did he. When she turned a corner, he sped up behind her and suddenly grabbed her shoulder to control her movement. In that moment, Leila had no choice: She was alone, he had made physical contact, and there was no one nearby to help. Her body kicked into fight mode, but she used it with control. She twisted out of his grip, drove her knee into his groin, and shouted, "Back off!" As he doubled over, she ran into a corner store just a few feet away and immediately called a friend. What made this an effective fight response wasn't just that she fought back; it's that she had already assessed her surroundings. She knew there was a clear exit nearby. There was no time to deescalate verbally, there was no one around to intervene, and not being assertive would have put her at more risk. Leila used the fight response not to "win" the encounter but to create enough disruption to escape. She acted fast, she created space, and she got to safety. That's what strategic fight mode looks like: rooted in awareness, intention, and a plan to get out.

Reaction Two: Flight Mode

Flight is your instinct to get out, to remove yourself from danger as quickly as possible. When done with intention, flight is often one of the safest and most effective self-defense strategies. It can deescalate a situation before it becomes violent. But like any response, it needs to be paired with awareness. If you're not grounded or paying attention to your surroundings, flight can lead you somewhere even less safe: a dark alley, a dead end, or a space with no one around. Sometimes the fear takes over and your body just wants to move, but that movement doesn't always lead to safety. That's why the goal isn't merely to *run* but also to *escape smart*. You don't need to have every step mapped out, but you do need to pause long enough to make sure you're heading somewhere that increases your chances of safety, not decreases them.

✕ Ineffective Flight Response

Hanna was walking home late at night when a man approached her with unsettling questions, asking her where she lived and if she wanted to go out with him. As she felt the situation become uncomfortable, she decided to avoid confrontation and hurriedly crossed the street into a more isolated area. The man, seeing her attempt to escape, followed her. Despite feeling increasingly unsafe, Hanna kept walking faster, avoiding eye contact. Eventually the man grabbed her arm and tried to drag her into the dark alley where she'd unintentionally led him. Hanna's decision to flee, while instinctual, had not been a well-thought-out choice because it led her further into danger. In this case, flight wasn't enough, and the lack of a plan or an awareness of the potential risks made her vulnerable.

✔ Effective Flight Response

Zahra was on the train when a man who had been making comments earlier followed her off at her stop. The second she noticed, she stayed calm and shifted course. Instead of heading to her usual exit, she walked quickly toward a nearby convenience store with bright lights and people inside. She took out her phone, ready to call for help if needed, and made it clear she was alert and watching. When the man kept pace behind her, she ducked into the store and asked the cashier if she could wait there a minute. Zahra's flight response wasn't just about leaving; it was about leaving smartly. She used her awareness to choose a safe, public place, and she took steps to protect herself along the way.

Reaction Three: Freeze Mode

Freezing is when your body shuts down and you go still, quiet, maybe even numb. It's your nervous system hitting pause when it doesn't know what else to do, mostly to protect your emotional well-being. But in many self-defense scenarios, freezing can leave you more vulnerable, especially if it keeps you from taking action when you have the chance. The freeze response is one of the most common reactions to fear or danger, yet it's the one people are most likely to feel ashamed about. In some situations, though, it can deescalate a confrontation before it turns violent. It can keep you from drawing attention to yourself in unsafe environments. It can buy you a few seconds to figure out what's happening and decide what to do next. For some survivors, freezing literally saved their lives. The problem isn't the freeze itself; it's when we get stuck in it, or when we internalize it as failure.

✕ Ineffective Freeze Response

Maya had been dating someone for a few months when, during a heated argument in a home with many people, he suddenly grabbed her and pinned her against the wall. Her body shut down. She couldn't think, scream, or fight back; she just froze. Even though she knew she needed to move, her body wouldn't let her. She stayed still, hoping it would be over soon. Eventually he let go, but the moment left a deep impact because it normalized this harm toward her and she felt bad for not responding. Maya's freeze response wasn't a failure; it was a protective reflex. But in that moment, it also left her completely vulnerable and unable to act.

✔ Effective Freeze Response

A similar situation happened to Isa. Her partner became aggressive and shoved her during an argument. The freeze hit fast, and her body locked up. But she recognized it. She had learned in her self-defense workshops that freezing didn't mean she was weak or broken. It just meant her body needed a second. Isa used that brief pause to take a deep breath, center herself, and then push her partner away. She didn't stay stuck. She created space, left the room, and called someone she trusted. The freeze reaction still affected her, but she didn't let it keep her from acting. She gave herself permission to move *after* the freeze. That shift from being frozen to choosing what's next is powerful.

Reaction Four: Fawn Mode

Fawning is when you try to appease, please, or accommodate someone who is hurting, threatening, or intimidating you not because you want to engage but because you're trying to keep the peace and stay safe. It's the *let me just make this* *better* instinct. But here's the thing: Fawning doesn't always protect you. Sometimes it actually invites more harm. When we default to appeasement, we can unintentionally reinforce power dynamics that make the other person feel more in control or more dominant, like they can push boundaries without consequences. And the more we fawn, the harder it becomes to recognize our own discomfort and set clear boundaries. It can keep us stuck in cycles of harm, especially in abusive relationships, workplaces, or even day-to-day interactions where we're constantly overaccommodating others to avoid tension. The goal isn't to shame yourself for fawning; it's to recognize when it's happening and slowly build the tools to respond differently, when it's safe to do so.

✕ Ineffective Fawn Response

One evening, Sherouk's partner became upset over something minor and began yelling. As the argument escalated, Sherouk instinctively tried to calm him down by apologizing repeatedly and offering to do whatever he wanted, even though she knew she hadn't done anything wrong. Her fawning behavior, trying to please him and avoid further confrontation, only made things worse. He saw her submission as a sign of weakness and became more aggressive. Instead of deescalating the situation, her fawning response allowed him to assert more control over her, making it harder for her to assert her own needs. Over time, this response became automatic, reinforcing the power imbalance in their relationship and escalating the emotional and physical violence that she faced. For years she existed in this abusive cycle and felt herself becoming smaller and smaller.

✔ Effective Fawn Response

Lila was in a similar situation. Her partner had a pattern: When things didn't go his way, he'd get verbally aggressive. In the past, she would fawn to avoid escalation. She'd agree with him, lower her voice, or take the blame just to keep the peace. But this time she noticed it happening in real time. She felt that instinct rise, the one that said, *Just smooth this over. Keep him calm.* Instead, she paused. Took a breath. Then said, clearly and calmly: "I'm not going to let you speak to me like that." Her partner's response? He exploded. Yelled louder. Punched a wall. The energy in the room shifted from tension to outright threat. This is the reality some people face when they stop fawning: The other person escalates. That doesn't mean the boundary was wrong; it means the environment was unsafe. Lila knew this. She had a plan. She didn't argue back. She grabbed her keys and left. She had already talked to a friend who told her she could crash there anytime. She took that offer. Later, she decided to get support and resources to exit this unsafe cycle.

Reaction Five: Flop Mode

Flopping is when your body or mind completely shuts down. You go limp. You dissociate. This is not the same as freezing, which is a pause in which you are alert but still. Flopping is what happens when your system short-circuits. You're not trying to soothe or fix. You're just . . . gone. Flopping happens when your nervous system decides that you can't run, can't fight, and can't reason with the threat. So instead, it shuts you down. It's a trauma response, often linked to tonic immobility or deep dissociation. For people who have experienced prolonged or repeated abuse, flopping can become the body's default way of surviving. It can be incredibly useful because when the nervous system detects that resistance might make things worse, flopping kicks in to reduce pain, limit visibility, and preserve life. It creates just enough disconnection for someone to emotionally survive what's happening.

✗ Ineffective Flop Response

During a team meeting, Maya's manager snapped at her in front of everyone for a small mistake on a report. The tone was sharp, humiliating, and completely out of proportion. The room went silent. Maya felt her body tense, and then everything inside her went slack. She didn't just freeze, as she had when her partner pushed her. This time she flopped. Her shoulders dropped, her mind fogged, and her notes blurred on the page. She stared down, nodded slowly, and went completely quiet, not because she was deciding what to do but because she wasn't really *there* anymore. She had checked out. It was like her brain pulled the emergency brake and left her running on autopilot. Afterward, a coworker gently asked if she was okay. Maya smiled and said, "Yeah, it's fine," without thinking. But inside she felt hollow, like her voice had been vacuumed out of her. She didn't feel like she *could* advocate for herself or report what happened. Her body had gone into shutdown mode to protect her from the emotional hit. But the cost was heavy: She left that meeting not just silenced but also disconnected from her own power. Flopping didn't feel like freezing or pausing. It felt like disappearing. And the more it happened, the more she started to believe that maybe disappearing was safer than being seen at all.

✔ Effective Flop Response

Tania had lived through trauma before, so when her boss slammed a door and started yelling about a missed deadline, she felt her brain start to fog. Her body froze, but not the kind of freeze where you're assessing. This was full-on collapse mode. She stopped making eye contact. She nodded silently. Her voice disappeared. Her body wanted nothing more than to shrink into the wall and vanish. But in that moment, something clicked. Because of therapy and healing spaces, she realized: *This is my flop response.* She didn't force herself to speak up. She didn't try to fix the situation. Instead, she gave herself permission to survive the moment. Later, when she got to the bathroom, she closed the stall, took a deep breath, and grounded herself. That night, she wrote down everything that happened. She called a close friend. And when she got home, she processed the experience in her journal and brought it up the next day in therapy, a space she'd already been using to heal from past trauma and learn how to recognize these flop patterns. With her therapist's support, she made a plan to document the behavior and bring it up with human resources. Tania didn't stop herself from flopping. The power came from recognizing the response, honoring it, and moving through it with intention once she was safe. She didn't judge her body. She didn't rush to perform strength. She used the tools she had—therapy, support, her own growing awareness—and took one grounded step forward at a time.

WHEN WE ENCOUNTER a threat, our brain kicks into survival mode and sends out a signal to the rest of the body: *Do something.* This is biology. It comes from an evolutionary blueprint. Fight, flight, freeze, fawn, and flop are automatic responses that helped our ancestors survive saber-toothed tigers and help us survive public transport delays and aggressive emails today. We also learn them over time, often through trauma, life under patriarchy, or just years of being told how to behave.

None of these is a weakness. I'm convinced one reason New Yorkers are seen as so intense is that we're subconsciously always scanning for threat. We are *ready*. Our modes aren't always pure nature; sometimes it's a result of our nervous system having been trained by living in a world that demands it. Whether we're walking through a crowded subway station or just trying to buy pizza without getting harassed, we're navigating threat responses all day. Again, the goal isn't to get rid of these responses. The goal is to understand them so you can use them as part of your self-defense toolkit. So when something goes down, you're not just reacting; you're *choosing*. You're not stuck in autopilot. You know what tools you have and when to use them. That's how we build a self-defense mindset.

BELIEVING IN YOUR POWER

OKAY, SO WE'VE talked about awareness, trauma responses, boundaries, and even why you should maybe look up from your phone once in a while (I say this with mad love). There's one last thing we need to land on: Believe in your personal power. Is it here with you? As I mentioned earlier, I always ask this in my self-defense classes: "Who here has a powerful body?" And almost every time, people look around like I must be talking to someone else. "Who can imagine themselves fighting back?" Crickets. Most of us have been taught to see our bodies as something to manage, hide, or control, not as something strong. Not as something worthy of defense, let alone capable of defending.

If you can't believe in your ability to protect yourself, it's going to be a whole lot harder to actually do it. Self-defense isn't just about knowing what to do; it's also about believing you can do something. It's about interrupting that voice that says "I could never" and replacing it with "Actually, I could." Because to act strategically, not automatically, you must believe that you've got power. Real power. Even if it's still waking up inside you.

I'll never forget one particular workshop on this subject.

I'm in Bogotá, Colombia, in 2018. A friend of mine has organized a gathering of feminist organizers, movement builders, and community protectors, the kind of people who make you sit up a little straighter when they walk into a room. They've come together for a self-defense class I'm teaching that evening, and I'm sweating through my shirt in a stale room full of plastic chairs and fluorescent lighting that hums louder than I'd like. It's not glamorous, but these women? They are powerhouses.

Before class starts, we do introductions. They tell me

about their work, organizing massive marches, running shelters, protecting survivors of trafficking, navigating threats from the state and nonstate actors alike. Some of them have faced violence on the front lines of protests. Some have literally smuggled women and children to safety. I'm sitting there taking notes like I'm interviewing them for a documentary. I'm in awe. Full fan-girl mode but trying not to look it.

Then we start. I open the session: "*¿Quién aquí tiene un cuerpo poderoso?* Who here has a powerful body?"

Not a single hand goes up.

I try again: "Who here thinks they could fight someone off if they had to?"

Still nada.

The silence is deep. And not because they're timid. I mean, come on. They face danger for a living. But when it comes to seeing their own bodies as powerful, as worthy of defense, something gets stuck. Eventually Beatrice, a reproductive justice activist who had just told me about risking her life to hide survivors, breaks the silence with a nervous laugh.

"*Tal vez podría gritar . . . pero pelear-pelear? No.* Maybe I could scream . . . but *fight* fight? No."

Then it hits me. These women, who do the kind of work that would intimidate most people, don't see themselves as physically strong. They've been taught to fight for others. But not for themselves. This is not unusual. Most people walk into self-defense spaces carrying shame or doubt. They assume they'll fail. That they'll freeze. That they're not "that type": not athletic, not tough, not aggressive enough. Listen, I get it. We're taught to be kind, to be small, to deescalate, to disappear. It makes sense that the idea of fighting back, physically, loudly, confidently, feels unthinkable.

So we get to work. I break down some basic techniques: stances, strikes, blocks, escapes. Nothing fancy. Just the foundation. And something starts to shift in the room. Laughter. Focus. Curiosity. They start coaching each other. Cheering each other on. And Beatrice? The one who swore she couldn't fight? She's the first one to volunteer to demonstrate a wrist release. And when she breaks free of the grip, she lets out this wild, joyful scream that makes the whole room erupt. That's her fight. Not just the technique, but the moment she believes she can do it.

By the end of class, the energy has completely changed. I ask again, "¿Quién tiene un cuerpo poderoso?" This time every hand flies up. No hesitation. Just power. They've always been fighters; they just hadn't seen their physical strength as part of that story until now.

Deescalate with Your Voice and Body

AS A REMINDER: Self-defense is deeply context-specific. Because you learned a technique in a calm, controlled environment, it's not always going to land the same way when your heart is racing, the streetlights are flickering, and someone is yelling in your face. The way you respond has to match the situation you're in. And if you're not tuned in to the context, if you're too focused on "doing it right" instead of reading the moment, you might end up in more danger, not less. That's why the answer to most questions in my classes is: it depends. You're the only person who can make the assessment about how best to respond to an escalated situation to create safety for yourself in that moment. No one understands that context better.

That's why in some of my classes I run this one exercise that tries to simulate that chaos. I have people step on each other's toes in pairs. Adrenaline starts rushing. People bump into walls, forget which side their dominant hand is on, totally blank. And that's the point: to show that practicing in a green zone, when you're calm and grounded, is not the same as reacting in a red zone, when your nervous system is in full-blown survival mode. The exercise is meant to simulate a bit of the chaos of the red zone.

So maybe you've got a perfect knee strike. Great. But in real life? The best move might be yelling. Or freezing strategically. Or deescalating. Or exiting. Self-defense isn't about memorizing moves; it's about having a toolbox and knowing when to use what.

Let me give you an example.

I was teaching a class the other day and shared a story from one of the first times a student ever called me after using what she learned. She was a Muslim woman who had attended a workshop I taught in Brooklyn. One night, after a long shift, she was walking to her car when a man started following her, yelling, getting louder, closer. She tried to ignore him. Crossed the street. He followed. Then he cut in front of her and reached out to grab her. She stomped her Doc Martens straight into his kneecaps, exactly like we practiced, and it worked. He buckled.

Except... self-defense in real life is chaotic; it's not clean or choreographed. It is full of split-second decisions. She turned to run, and just like that, he grabbed her from behind as soon as he had the chance to. She had to improvise and use everything she could think of and all of her strength to fight back. Some of it she learned in our class and some of it was instinctive. Most importantly, she was able to make it out.

This story is a reminder that self-defense isn't just about

memorizing a script of techniques; context matters. Only you can decide how to use your voice and your mind to make your best move and get yourself to safety.

STRATEGIC EXIT IS SELF-DEFENSE

IF THINGS ARE getting heated, especially in a public verbal situation, and you have a safe way to step away, do it. You don't have to engage. Leaving can be the smartest and safest move. If nothing is physical yet and you don't anticipate physicality in the situation, you can exit in a way that makes sense to the situation. If the situation is already physically escalating but you've created an opening, what's the most strategic way to exit? After you've created an opening, whether through a strike, a yell, a block, or a distraction, your instinct might be to run, but the smarter move is to sidestep around the person without turning your back. Keep your eyes on them and be careful not to trip. You might need to reinforce your opening, so yell again, strike again. You need to know if they're still a threat: Are they getting up? Reaching for something? Following you? If you turn around too soon, you lose that visibility and give them the advantage. Stay low, keep your stance strong, and use your voice, yelling commands like "Back off!" or "Get away from me!" to both disorient the attacker and alert others around you. You're shielding the most vulnerable parts of your body: your face, your throat, your core. It's your *get-the-hell-out-of-here* stance. Look for a clear and safe exit, toward light, people, stores, or traffic, not isolation. Keep scanning your surroundings, and once you've created enough distance and feel confident the threat is neutralized or no longer advancing, then you turn and move quickly or use the movement technique outlined below, what I call the eyes-up exit. Your goal isn't to win; it's to survive, and to do that, you must leave with your eyes open, your awareness sharp, and your body still in control. Simply walking away might work, but not always.

So you sidestep. Think salsa, not sprint. Move at a diagonal, keeping your body turned slightly sideways, so your arms stay between you and the threat. The goal is to move around them without ever giving them a clean shot at your back. Once you're at a safe distance, *then*, and only then, do you turn and move fast.

When you're grounded and in a safe space, take a breath. Let your nervous system catch up. Document what happened. Write it down while the memory is fresh: what the person looked like, what they were wearing, the time, the place, exactly what was said or done. Even if you don't want to report it right away, having a record matters. Finally, don't carry it alone. Tell someone. A friend, a loved one, a therapist, a community member, someone who can hold the weight with you.

VERBAL DEESCALATION IS SELF-DEFENSE

IN ONE OF my classes, someone raised their hand and asked, "What if I can't leave? What if I'm stuck and someone's getting in my face?" It's a real question and one I hear a lot. Because sometimes the option to exit just doesn't exist. You might be on a crowded train, in a narrow hallway, or in a space where walking away could actually make things more dangerous. Sometimes the smartest next thing you can do is nothing at all. If someone's yelling from across the street or tossing words your way on the train and you can safely ignore it, that's power. You don't owe anyone your energy. But there are moments when silence isn't enough, and then your voice becomes your next line of defense. Verbal deescalation isn't about clapping back or meeting aggression with aggression. It's about using your tone, words, and body language to shift the energy, draw a boundary, or buy yourself enough time to move to safety.

There are two main ways we use our voice in self-defense: verbal fawning and verbal fighting. Neither one is about being passive or aggressive. Both are about being strategic. They're tools we use depending on the moment, the energy in the situation, and what will keep us safe.

Verbal fawning is a self-defense tactic that uses calm, nonconfrontational language and body cues to deescalate a situation when things feel like they might spiral. It's not about being submissive or agreeable; it's about being smart and strategic with your energy. Think of it as emotional aikido: You're redirecting the momentum, not absorbing it. You're lowering the tension in the room without shrinking yourself. You're staying in control by not becoming a threat.

It can look like softening your tone, avoiding direct eye contact, having your hands visible, and keeping your posture relaxed. It can sound like any of these: "I hear you. I'm not trying to cause any problems." "Totally get it — you're right." "I respect that. Let's both take a second."

When you use this kind of language, you're sending a clear message: *I'm not a threat. I'm not here to challenge you. I'm trying to get out of this situation safely and peacefully.* That doesn't mean you're scared or incapable of stepping up, pushing back, meeting the energy with the same energy. It means you're smart. You're choosing a response that lowers the risk of escalation, especially when the person in front of you is looking for a fight, control, or a reaction. You're taking power back, not by matching their energy but by disarming it.

I've used this many times in street harassment situations, in tense rooms where I was the only woman, in moments where someone else's rage was clearly not about me but could still land on me. For example, one time on the subway, someone shoved into me and then turned around and snapped, "Why did you push me?" My whole body went tense. I knew I hadn't pushed them, but I also knew arguing wasn't going to get me anywhere. So I took a breath and said calmly, "Sorry, I didn't mean to." That was it. I didn't meet their energy. I didn't try to prove I was right. I just let it land lightly, and he moved on. It wasn't about agreeing with him; it was about ending it. I chose the response that kept me safe, not the one that satisfied my ego.

Verbal fawning is especially useful when...

You're physically cornered or outnumbered.

The person feels unpredictable or unstable.

You can't exit safely.

You need to buy time or redirect attention.

Verbal fawning is not helpful when...

The person has already become physically violent.

Fawning has been used repeatedly in a pattern of
ongoing abuse.

It's escalating the situation further, not deescalating.

Now let's say that moment on the subway didn't end there. Let's say they didn't back down after I said, "Sorry, I didn't mean to." Let's say they kept coming at me louder, closer, angrier, breathing on me, getting into my space. That's when I have to shift. That's when verbal fawning is no longer enough, and I move into what I call verbal force.

Verbal force is not about screaming or losing control. It's about being assertive, grounded, and crystal clear in your boundaries. It's when you use your voice, not to deescalate through compliance but to interrupt and claim space. You're no longer trying to calm the situation; you're now making it known that the behavior is not okay and that you are not going to accept it. If they had escalated in the subway, I would have used a firm, calm tone and said something like "Step away. I don't know you. Do not yell at me," all while holding my palms out to create visible space. It's not just about the words. It's also about the delivery. Your body language, your eye contact, the steadiness of your voice—all of these things work together to send a message: *You're not going to mess with me.*

If verbal fawning is about redirecting someone's energy, then verbal force is about blocking the energy. This is when your tone changes. Your body shifts. Your words get short, clear, and carry weight. You're not negotiating anymore. You're not playing small. It's the self-defense version of a mic drop: no extra words, no apologies, just truth, volume, and boundaries delivered with clarity and control. Verbal force might sound like: "Back off. I said no." "Step away from me." "I don't know you. Leave me alone." "Stop touching me."

Verbal force is especially useful when...

You're in a public or semipublic space where others can witness or help.

Someone is pushing past your verbal boundaries.

You need to interrupt escalating behavior or buy time to exit.

You've already tried deescalation and it didn't work.

Verbal force is not helpful when...

The person has a weapon and you're isolated.

You're physically restrained or cornered with no safe exit.

You're in a coercive, long-term abusive situation.

Your body is in a freeze response and speech isn't
accessible.

One of the most effective verbal force tools is what I call "name-and-claim." This tactic is all about being specific. You name exactly what is happening, who is doing it, and what you need, and you say it out loud, clearly, and without hesitation. The goal is twofold: first, to make the aggressor visible and accountable, and second, to activate bystanders who may be unsure or frozen. When people hear something specific, like what behavior is happening and who it's coming from, they're far more likely to step in.

Here's what name-and-claim sounds like in action. Let's say you're on the subway and someone touches you inappropriately. Instead of just saying "Can you please stop," which could be brushed off or ignored, you say, "Person in the red shirt, get your hand off me. I do not know you." Then you shift to others around you: "Person in the pink shirt, can you help me? I need help now." You've just done three things: named the harm, claimed your right to safety, and pulled someone into a position of support. This tactic is especially useful in public or semipublic places, such as a bus, a side-walk, or a party, where there are people around but the social dynamics might still keep them silent. Name-and-claim cuts through that silence.

The second tactic, called "broken record," is for situations where someone keeps testing your boundary, over and over. Maybe they keep asking for your number, inching into your personal space, or pretending they didn't hear you the first time you said no. This technique gives you a way to hold your boundary without getting pulled into a debate, explanation, or emotional tug-of-war. The idea is simple: Pick a clear statement and repeat it. Calmly. Firmly. As many times as it takes. Here's what that could sound like: You're seated and someone keeps pressuring you to talk. You respond: "I'm not interested." They push again. You say: "Have a good day." They try to joke about it, guilt-trip you, or ask again. You repeat: "Have a good day. Have a good day. Have a good day." The power of this tactic is that it gives the aggressor nothing new to grab on to. No fresh emotion. No argument to counter. No energy to feed off. Just your no. This tactic is useful in both public and private settings, on the street, in a workplace, or even with someone you know, anytime someone is trying to wear you down through persistence.

No matter which verbal force tactic you're using, whether you're calling out someone specifically or repeating yourself like a broken record, what makes it truly effective is how you anchor it. Your words alone aren't always enough; it's the way you say them, the way you hold your body, the energy you bring into the room. When you stand with your feet grounded, shoulders back, hands ready, voice clear and steady, you're not just speaking; you're holding a boundary. You don't need to shout to be powerful, but you do need to be firm. A shaky "Please don't" lands very differently than a rooted "Stop. Now." And that difference can shift the entire energy of a moment.

Take it from one of our Malikah elders, a woman who's been a force in Queens way before the borough was cool. A few years ago, after a protest in our neighborhood, she was driving home when a police officer pulled her over and demanded she get out of the car. She'd taken one of our self-defense classes, and she remembered what we teach. So when this officer leaned in, trying to escalate, she didn't argue. She didn't flinch. She just looked at him and repeated, in her Egyptian-accented English, clear as day, "Have a good day. Have a good day. Have a good day." Like a mantra. Like she was sending him on his way with nothing but grace and a boundary he couldn't cross. And you know what? It worked. He eventually gave up, stepped back, and let her drive away. Someone caught the whole thing on video, and when I saw it, I teared up. Watching an immigrant, hijab-wearing Muslim woman hold that kind of line, in public, with nothing but her voice and her presence, felt like witnessing something sacred. She didn't raise her voice. She just refused to be moved. And that's Queens. That's power. That's self-defense.

If you're not used to being loud, assertive, or commanding, using your voice to deescalate, whether through verbal fawning or verbal force, can feel nearly impossible. It's not just about volume. It's about having the permission to take up space, to be firm, to say exactly what you want. And for many of us, that kind of permission was never given. If you weren't socialized to fight and if your body learned early on to freeze in moments of conflict, then it makes sense that your voice might disappear when you need it most (this is why safety whistles are popular). That isn't failure. That's your nervous system just trying to survive. So give yourself grace. You're not doing it wrong; you just haven't had the chance to practice.

In my classes I do an exercise where I line people up in two rows across from each other. One partner walks forward, and the other's only job is to say one word: "Stop." Every single time, the room bursts into giggles. Nervous, bubbling, contagious laughter. At first I was with it, the joy, the silliness, the lightness of it all. But over time, the laughter started to hit differently. It made me sad. Because beneath those giggles was something deeper: How foreign, how uncomfortable, how unpracticed it feels for so many of us to assert ourselves, even when we're standing in safety, in the green zone, surrounded by support.

It usually takes seven, eight, sometimes ten tries before

everyone can get their body and voice to work together, before they can say "Stop" with clarity, with purpose, and with conviction. That's the truth about assertiveness. It's about practicing. It's a muscle, and like any other muscle, you have to train it. Verbal technique is one of the most important parts of self-defense, and—let's be real—it's also the part that feels the most awkward at first. You're in your room alone, yelling "Stop!" into the air. But you've got to train your body and your voice to work together so that when it matters, your words come out clear, confident, and without hesitation.

Here's how I tell folks to start: Picture a situation where someone's crossing your boundary, getting too close, not letting up. Write down what you'd say. Maybe it's "No," "Leave me alone," or "Back up. I said no." Then actually say it out loud. Don't just think it. Say it like you're on that subway platform and you mean it. Say it again. Say it louder. Practice until it feels less like a performance and more like a reflex.

THE MORE YOU practice using your voice, the more you realize it's also about activating the people around you. Self-defense doesn't have to be a solo mission. Sometimes the most powerful thing you can do is pull folks in, call for help, break the silence. However, in our individualistic, lonely world today, people don't always jump in, even when they know they should. That's the bystander effect, everyone waiting for someone else to be brave first.

So here's where we're headed next: How do we break that collective freeze? How do we shift a crowd from silence to action? Because safety isn't just personal, it's collective. And building a culture where people actually show up for one another? That's the truest form of safety.

THE BYSTANDER EFFECT

IT WAS A cold night in March 1964 when twenty-eight-year-old Kitty Genovese was walking home after a late bartending shift. She parked her car just down the block from her apartment in Kew Gardens, Queens, and started off on a short walk she had probably made dozens of times before. But this time, as she headed toward her building, she was attacked from behind by a man named Winston Moseley. He stabbed her. She screamed, loud, terrified, begging for help. Lights turned on in nearby windows. People heard her. Some even looked out. But no one came. She managed to get up and stumble toward her building. Moseley ran off and then came back. This time he raped her. Then stabbed her again, killing her just outside her apartment. The whole thing lasted about thirty minutes. And according to the original *New York Times* report, thirty-eight people saw or heard part of it. One neighbor later said, "I didn't want to get involved."

When the *New York Times* ran the headline "37 Who Saw Murder Didn't Call the Police," the country was horrified.

But for many of us, especially survivors, it doesn't feel that surprising. We know what it's like to be in danger while the world watches and stays silent. We know what it's like to scream and not be believed.

In the 1960s, the story lit a fire under two social psychologists at Columbia, Bibb Latané and John Darley, who began to study what became known as the bystander effect, the phenomenon where the more people witness harm, the less likely any one person is to intervene. And here's why that matters for us: When we talk about self-defense, we're not just talking about individual moves or personal strength. We're talking about what it takes to create communities where safety is shared, where harm is interrupted, where people know how to show up for each other and choose to. That's what we need for true safety.

Latané and Darley set up a series of studies to explore how people respond to crisis, and why so many of us freeze when it's time to act on behalf of others. In the first study, participants were told they were helping with a research project, and suddenly they overheard what sounded like someone in another room having a seizure. If they thought they were the only one who could help, 85 percent jumped in. But when they believed two other people were also listening? That dropped to 64 percent. And when they thought four other people were around? Only 31 percent responded.

The more people in the room, the less likely anyone was to do anything. Then they ran another experiment. This time, participants were put in a room to complete a task, and a few minutes in, smoke began to creep under the door. Thick, black smoke. If they were alone, 75 percent reported it. But if they were sitting with others who didn't react, only 10 percent did anything. Even with literal smoke filling the room, people looked around, saw everyone else frozen, and took that as a cue to stay silent. This is what they called pluralistic ignorance, when we don't trust our own instincts because no one else is moving. We tell ourselves: *If this were really a big deal, wouldn't someone else be stepping in?* That instinct to freeze, to defer, to wait for someone else is at the heart of the bystander effect. And it's not just academic. It shows up in real life all the time: when someone's being harassed on the train, when a friend says something harmful at a party, when violence unfolds in plain sight and no one steps in. Not because they don't care, but because no one has taught them how.

Before we run with the idea that people never intervene, let's complicate it. Based on decades of research, we know that the bystander effect is real, but the story that helped define it, the murder of Kitty Genovese, wasn't as simple as the headlines made it seem. The claim that thirty-eight people saw or heard her being attacked and did nothing?

It was exaggerated. Some people called the police. Others didn't fully understand what was happening. And the way the media framed the story, a white woman attacked in a quiet, middle-class Queens neighborhood, stoked public fear and helped justify a wave of racist policing strategies that reshaped the city. But beyond the numbers and the headlines, there's a harder truth we have to sit with: When people do choose to act, they're not acting for everyone equally. Research shows we're more likely to intervene for people we relate to, people we see as sympathetic, familiar, or worthy of help. In a 2011 meta-analysis, researchers actually reviewed fifty-eight studies on the bystander effect to better understand the factors influencing whether individuals intervene in emergencies. They found that helping behavior was more likely when bystanders felt a personal connection to the victim. That matters. Because if safety is extended only to some, it's not real safety. It's bias dressed up as instinct. And here's what I've seen in communities across the world: The bystander effect doesn't have to be the norm. In many global majority contexts, and right here in working-class and poor neighborhoods in the United States, people don't wait to be told to intervene. They just *do*. On Steinway Street, right outside the Malikah Safety Center, if voices start to rise, suddenly five people are crowding around, trying to deescalate the situation, calm things down, figure out who said what. No one minds their own business, and honestly, that's part of what keeps us safe. I once saw a street fight in Egypt where there was an intense physical struggle unfolding and still people jumped in to stop the conflict. No hesitation. No silence. Just community, messy and involved. Which tells us something important: The bystander effect isn't fixed. It's shaped by culture, by values, by how we've been trained to respond to each other. And if it's shaped, it can be reshaped. We can learn to move and to show up when it counts.

HOW TO NOT JUST STAND THERE

WE'VE BEEN TALKING about the bystander effect, that moment when something's going down and everyone freezes, waiting for someone else to act. And one thing I always hear in class, without fail, is: "Should I yell 'fire' instead of 'help'?" I get why people ask. There's this old myth that yelling "fire" is more effective because it triggers self-interest: People might ignore someone yelling "help," but they'll respond to a threat that might affect them. But let's be super honest: If I hear "fire" anywhere, I'm not rushing to help, because I'm sprinting in the opposite direction. "Fire" creates panic. It confuses people. It doesn't tell anyone what's actually happening or what you need from them. If you want to cut through that bystander effect, you've got to be clear and direct. That's where name-and-claim and broken record come in: two simple strategies, as we've already discussed, that make people around you move.

Picture this: You're on a crowded train and someone grabs you. Instead of just yelling "stop" or "help," you say: "Person in the black shirt, can you help me?" Or "You in the red hoodie, I'm being attacked. Please help me." You're not just shouting into the void. You're naming what's happening and assigning responsibility. So now what do you do when you witness harm happening to someone else?

You know that itch in your gut that says something's not right but you're not sure how to act without making things worse? When we witness violence, harassment, or injustice, the impulse to act is powerful. But not every moment is ours to intervene directly, and not every action helps the person at the center. The question isn't just "What can I do?" It's "What does support look like for them, and is it safe to offer it?" Using a framework created by the organization Right to Be, here are five ways to assess what kind of intervention is possible, depending on the situation.

1. Direct (When It's Safe to Do So)

Use this when someone is facing verbal harassment or bullying and it's clear that stepping in won't escalate the harm.

What it looks like: Face the person being targeted: "Are you okay?" Then, if safe, interrupt the aggressor: "That's not okay. Leave them alone." The goal is not to perform heroism; it's to offer support, safety, and solidarity in real time.

2. Distract (When Confrontation Could Escalate)

Use this when tension is high, like street harassment or a controlling situation, and calling out the aggressor could make things worse.

What it looks like: Create a subtle interruption. Ask the person being targeted for directions, drop your keys, or strike up an unrelated conversation. Distraction works by giving the person being targeted a chance to move, breathe, or reset, without escalating the aggressor.

3. Document (When You Can't Step In Safely)

Sometimes the safest and most powerful way to support someone is by bearing witness, especially when they're up against power (like police or abusive authority).

What it looks like: Use your phone to film discreetly. Take detailed notes. Stay focused on the person experiencing harm. If possible, ask afterward: "Would you like this footage?" Always ask before sharing publicly. Documentation is about their needs, not going viral.

4. Delegate (When You Can't Act Alone)

Use this when someone is being physically intimidated or harmed and you don't have the capacity to intervene directly.

What it looks like: Get help. Find someone with power in the space — a transit worker, teacher, security staff, manager — and say, "That person needs support." You can also ask other bystanders to act with you. Together is safer.

5. Delay (When the Situation Is Too Risky to Intervene Immediately)

Some forms of violence, especially intimate partner violence or abuse behind closed doors, carry real danger if interrupted in the moment, so it could be better to intervene once the immediate harm has passed.

What it looks like: Check in later. Go up to the person experiencing the harm after the perpetrator has exited. Text. Call. Say: "I noticed what happened. I'm here if you want to talk. I can walk you somewhere if you need or help you report." Support doesn't expire when the harm ends. In fact, it might matter even more.

THERE ARE TIMES when you have to employ several of these strategies and times when you might choose not to intervene based on factors outside what I've mentioned. This is good to use as a framework as you begin to unlearn and push against a natural and individual inclination that produces the bystander effect. Intervening on behalf of others always carries the risk of violence redirected at you or further escalation. In the moment, you'll be the most equipped to assess which of these options you might use or if you won't intervene at all. Trust your gut and do what is safest for you in that moment.

Let me introduce you to Fahima. She's not just one person; she's a composite of so many of my students at Malikah, the kind who come to self-defense class with stories that make you pause, laugh, cry, and/or want to plot a revolution. Fahima is that caring, present friend who always notices what others miss. The one who asks, "Did you see that?" when someone gets shoved on the train, and you're still trying to figure out where the noise came from. She's quick-witted, kindhearted, and curious, always moving through the world with one eyebrow raised and one hand ready to help. She keeps a spare dollar tucked in her coat for whoever might need it. But she also knows not every moment is hers to intervene. She has learned how to read the room, assess the risk, and respond accordingly, which is what bystander intervention is all about: direct, distract, document, delegate, and delay. Fahima's just trying to be a decent human being in a hard world and stay safe doing it. She intervenes when she can, in ways that center the person experiencing harm, and she gives herself grace when she can't. So as we talk about these intervention strategies, Fahima will be our guide. Maybe you're her. Maybe you're becoming her, inshallah.

1. DIRECTLY ENGAGE: Engaging the Person Doing the Harm to Disrupt the Violence

Scenario

It's rush hour in New York City. Packed train. Nowhere to move. Fahima is standing near the subway doors. She notices a man standing too close to a woman nearby. Not just close, but pressing in. He's muttering under his breath, something crude, something that makes the woman shrink into herself. The woman scans the train with that look we all recognize: the quiet, desperate search for someone, anyone, to notice.

Fahima's Intervention

Because she is on a crowded subway train, Fahima decides to intervene directly. She steps forward and addresses the man loudly and firmly: "You're making her uncomfortable. Back off now." The man looks startled, stops his comments, and steps back. Fahima turns to the woman and asks if she's okay, making sure she feels safe and supported. The woman nods, relief in her eyes. Fahima stays with her through the next stop. They both get off together, safely.

Why Fahima Rocked

In this context, Fahima's direct confrontation stopped the harasser in his tracks. She wasn't aggressive in a way that escalated the scenario, but she was assertive enough to interrupt the behavior, drawing attention to it and creating a moment where the woman could feel protected. She assessed the risks and found that direct intervention was feasible because of the location of the incident.

2. DISTRACT: Engaging the Person Experiencing the Harm to Distract and Disrupt from the Violence

Scenario

It's early evening, and Fahima's walking home, tote bag slung over her shoulder, earbuds in but the volume low. That's just how she moves through the world—tuned in. She notices a woman ahead of her on the sidewalk. And behind that woman is a person, stumbling a little, slurring his words, shouting racist things at the woman. The woman speeds up. So does he. Fahima can feel her own pulse rising. She knows this could go south very fast.

Fahima's Intervention

Instead of confronting the man directly (which could escalate things, especially because the person does not appear to be sober and able to rationalize), Fahima uses distraction. Fahima checks in with the woman, sees if she's okay, and then, with her consent, directs her into the deli on the corner. She uses this moment to explain to the woman what she saw and recommends to her some resources to support her and where she can report this street harassment incident. Once the person has left the area, they step out of the deli and proceed on their own commutes.

Why Fahima Rocked

Fahima didn't call the man out. She *called in the woman*. She shifted the energy, not by escalating but by creatively disrupting the dynamic. That's distraction: helping some-one exit a dangerous or violating situation *without* directly engaging the aggressor. It's not about being sneaky. It's about being strategic. And Fahima nailed it, like those vid-eos where people burst into random song to interrupt a rac-ist rant or loudly ask for directions to confuse a harasser. The best distraction tactics are subtle, surprising, and safe. Fahima didn't just help the woman feel safer; she helped her feel *seen*. And sometimes that's the biggest disruption of all.

3. DELEGATE: Getting Help to Defuse the Situation, So You Don't Have to Be on Your Own

Scenario
Fahima's on the subway platform, waiting for the next train. She's scanning the tracks like every New Yorker does, half bored, half alert, when she hears yelling. She turns. Someone is shouting aggressively at a woman, shoving her, screaming for her to get out of his way. The woman looks terrified, cor-nered. It's escalating, fast, and the woman is alone and asking bystanders for help. People are hesitant to intervene.

Fahima's Intervention
Fahima's gut tells her this one's not safe to handle alone. She's not going to throw herself between them because the perpe-trator is being aggressive. She finds the nearest MTA worker in a neon vest just a few feet away and moves quickly: "Hi,

someone's being harassed on the platform. Can you help?" The MTA worker doesn't hesitate. The perpetrator is pulled aside. The woman is moved to a safer space away from the perpetrator. Fahima checks in and stays nearby to make sure the woman's okay, just in case she needs an ally when the adrenaline wears off.

Why Fahima Rocked

Fahima knew this wasn't her fight to take on solo. She didn't try to be a one-woman SWAT team. She assessed the risk, for herself and for the woman, and used the resources around her. That's delegation. It's one of the most underused but so *deeply powerful* tools in bystander intervention. Whether it's a guard, a store manager, a teacher, or a group of friends that is nearby, Fahima knows that the burden doesn't have to fall on one person's shoulders.

4. DELAY: Supporting the Person Experiencing the Harm After the Incident Is No Longer at Its Most Aggravated Point

Scenario

Fahima's sitting in a university seminar, half listening to a group discussion, when the perpetrator in the room starts going off. He's interrupting a woman repeatedly, rolling his eyes at her points, then drops a sexist comment about her appearance masked as a "joke." Classic microaggression, heavy on the aggression. The woman stiffens. Doesn't respond. There's an awkward silence in the room, then business as usual.

Fahima's Intervention

Fahima doesn't jump in mid-discussion. She knows that calling it out publicly right then might make the situation more uncomfortable, especially for the woman being targeted. She doesn't know the details or the nature of this relationship. So she waits. After class, once the perpetrator disappears, Fahima catches up to her classmate outside. "Hey, I saw what happened in there. That was way out of line. You didn't deserve that. Just wanted to say I've got your back if you ever want to talk or need backup addressing it. Is there anything you need?" She's casual but clear. Offering care, not pressure. She opens a door.

Why Fahima Rocked

Fahima understood that not every response needs to be in the heat of the moment. Sometimes people need space. Time. A chance to breathe and process before deciding what they want to do next. That's what delay is all about. It's not inaction; it's intentional action taken when the moment is safer, more grounded, and centered on what the person who experienced the harm actually wants. Fahima didn't speak for her classmate. She didn't swoop in to be the hero. She simply said: *I saw it. I'm here.* And sometimes that quiet, thoughtful follow-up is the moment that actually makes someone feel seen, maybe for the first time all day.

5. DOCUMENT: Recording to Disrupt Violence or to Collect Evidence for Proper Reporting Through Video, Writing, Photography

Scenario

Fahima works part-time at a coffee shop, and she notices the perpetrator, who is also her manager, making inappropriate comments to one of the younger employees. She's making suggestive remarks and is getting too touchy with her in front of the customers. Fahima sees the employee become visibly uncomfortable. She recognizes that there is a power dynamic at play and understands that the younger employee needs this job.

Fahima's Intervention

Fahima decides to document the harassment to protect the employee. She discreetly pulls out her phone and begins recording the interaction from a distance, making sure to capture the manager's comments and any inappropriate actions. Afterward, she gets permission from the employee who has been harmed to share the recording with human resources, encouraging the employee to speak up if she feels comfortable doing so, but also ensuring that the evidence is available should the employee need it later.

Why Fahima Rocked

By documenting the incident, Fahima ensures that there's a record of what happened, which can be vital for holding the manager accountable. She's also respecting the employee's agency, allowing her to make the decision on how to proceed without forcing her into any particular action. She gives the victim the choice of whether or not to share or use the video in any way. By creating accountability through community, she helped break a cycle of violence in isolation and make the world safer for everyone.

IF YOU'VE BEEN paying attention to Fahima, you've probably noticed that she's not a superhero. She's not flawless. But she pays attention. She trusts her gut, knows her options, and chooses the one that centers the person experiencing harm, whether that means stepping in loud and clear, throwing off a harasser with a fake deli run, or circling back hours later to say, "That wasn't okay and I've got you." Sometimes the move is direct. Sometimes it's quiet. Sometimes it's a well-timed side-eye and a sharp "Is there a reason you're still talking?" But the thread through all of it is presence. The world would be a safer place if more people spoke up when they saw violence unfold. That safer place is possible, but we can't do it alone.

Strike Back (Only If You Need To)

BY THE TIME you reach this point in the book, you've already learned how to read a room, trust your gut, use your voice, and call on your community. You've learned to exit, to hold boundaries even when it feels impolite, and to center your own safety (or the safety of the person experiencing violence, if you're in a situation where you're choosing to be an active bystander). Sometimes, even when you do everything "right," the violence doesn't stop. Sometimes it escalates quickly, physically, terrifyingly, and you find yourself face-to-face with the moment you hoped would never come. There might be a time when someone decides they don't care about your boundaries. When they push past your words, past your planning, past your exit. This is what we call the red zone. It's the moment when your nervous system kicks into overdrive, your heart races, and your body starts scanning for the next possible move. And in some cases — not most, but enough — the only available move left is to physically *fight back*.

In late 2023, the United Nations released a devastating report on femicide, the intentional killing of women for simply being women. On average, 140 women and girls are killed every day by a family member. That means every ten minutes, somewhere in the world, a woman is murdered by someone who was supposed to love her. Violence doesn't care what we're wearing. It doesn't care how kind we were, how many people were around, or whether we said no the right way. That's why this chapter exists. If you ever need to fight back, I want you to do so with everything you have — out of love for your own life and for the people in your life who love you too. That love is your fiercest weapon.

I know this from experience. Years ago, I was on a crowded subway in Istanbul with five friends, women I'd grown close to while we were there for a summer program. We were volunteering, teaching, taking classes, trying to learn a new city and contribute something to it. This was one of our rare days off, and we were excited to explore. I remember wearing a flowing polka-dot dress and a white scarf wrapped neatly around my head. I felt beautiful, and more importantly, I felt safe surrounded by women I trusted, in a crowd that felt neutral and ordinary. Safety is never guaranteed, not even in the daylight. As we stood talking, the metro doors closed behind us, and I suddenly felt something strange, a pressure, too close. I turned to find a man pressed up against me, his body violating mine in a way that was deliberate, disgusting, and unmistakably clear. Without hesitation, I turned and shouted: "Stop. Get back." My voice was loud, trained, intentional. But instead of backing off, he lunged forward, his face turning red, trying to silence me. That's when I pushed him again and again. Hard. I used both of my hands and shoved him again, harder, my voice getting louder: "Stop. Get back." My body remembered what it was supposed to do when someone refused to listen to my words. And when the doors opened for the next stop, I gave one final push and threw him out through the opening doors.

And then I broke. I had been violated. I felt like I wanted to unzip my own skin and escape myself. My hands, the same ones that defended me, felt covered in something I couldn't wash off. I wanted to scream and scrub and disappear. But I also felt relief. Relief that my body knew how to protect me. Relief that I was able to use my voice and my strength and that I was safe. That's what we prepare for. That's why we train. Not because we want to be violent, but because we want to be ready *if* violence is forced on us.

What's more, when we act to defend ourselves in a public space, it sends a message to others too. It communicates that violence is not okay. It communicates that I have the right to exist without fear, as does everybody. It communicates that my body and my space are mine to protect. I do not need to accept violence as it happens to me. If I'm experiencing violence, I will physically fight back.

Remember that when someone tries to physically hurt you, your response isn't always to start with a punch. Our goal is to deescalate, not escalate, and using a strike can lead to escalation if not used properly. You can generally assume that once you throw a strike, another one will be thrown back at you, hard. This is why striking is often our last step. We start with defense techniques. Blocking and grappling are your first physical tools in the fight for your safety. They are the skills that keep you upright when someone wants you down, and that free you when someone thinks they own your body.

Blocking is what you do when someone tries to hit you; it's the art of protecting yourself from impact. Grappling is what you do when someone grabs you. It's about reclaiming control when someone else has decided to take it. This isn't about brute force. This is about technique. It's about knowing how to move your wrist just enough to break a grip, how to shift your hips to undo a chokehold, how to use your center of gravity.

When I first started martial arts, blocks felt boring, to be honest. They weren't the high kicks or the knockout punches. But what I've learned, what I've lived, is that a block is one of the most impactful things your body can do. Here are the five foundational techniques I teach to begin reclaiming that power:

Defense from an arm grab
Defense from a neck grab
Defense from a back grab
Blocks from strikes
Defense on the ground

So before we learn how to strike, we learn how to stop the violence from landing. You are not a victim waiting to be hit. You are a force that knows how to hold the line.

1. When They Grab Your Wrist

Picture this: You're heading home after an event, or maybe you're just outside a store after grabbing a snack. Someone starts talking to you, and at first it's chill. You're in your green zone, casually chatting, nodding. But then something shifts. The questions start to corner you:

"Where do you live?"
"Why won't you smile?"
"Can I have your number?"

You turn to walk away, but before you can take two steps, they grab your wrist. And now you're in your red zone. Your body knows it. But you've been trained.

Step 1: Drop into your power stance

Plant your feet about shoulder width apart. One foot goes slightly in front of the other. Bend your front knee lightly to ground your stance. From here, it's harder for someone to pull you, you're in a more stable stance from which to pivot, and you're no longer giving them control. Think of this stance as the physical way of saying, I'M NOT GOING ANYWHERE I DON'T CHOOSE TO. Then start to rotate your wrist.

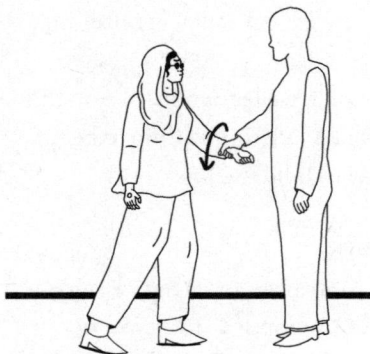

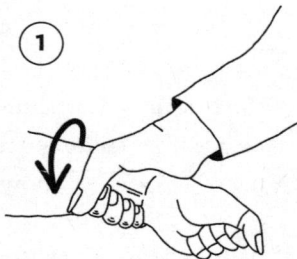

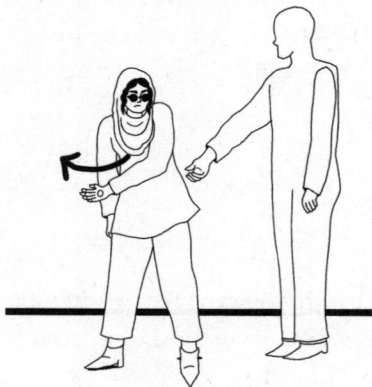

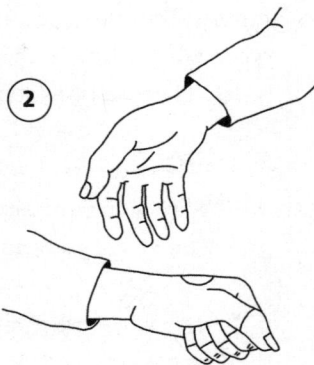

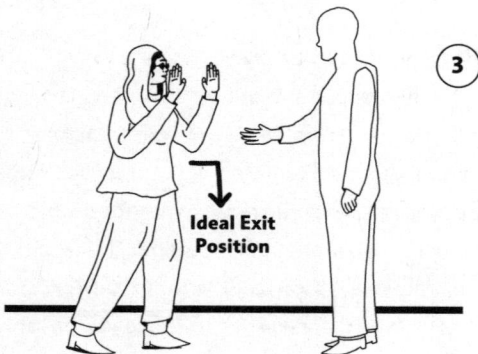

Ideal Exit Position

Step 2: Rotate your hand toward the thumb (not just with your wrist, use your hips)

Your first instinct might be to yank your arm straight back. Don't. That just makes you a tug-of-war rope. Instead, you're going to turn your wrist toward *their* thumb, which is the weakest part of their grip. But here's the secret: You're not just twisting your wrist. You're powering the whole movement from your hips. Pivot like you're trying to check your back pocket for your phone. Your wrist turns in toward your chest while your elbow lifts and pulls out from your body. The motion is sharp, controlled, and powered by your whole core.

Step 3: Create space

Once your wrist is free, don't just stand there. You need to act fast. Use your free hand to create distance by holding your arms up at a 45-degree angle in front of you. Make sure your elbows are tucked in and your palms are extended out to protect your core and face. This makes your body look bigger, keeps your guard up, and signals to everyone around that this interaction is not okay. You can use your voice and say what you need loud and clear: "Get back! Don't touch me!" "You're too close!"

Then exit fast. Now that you've disrupted their control, you need to remove yourself from the situation as soon as there is an opening. If you're still near the store, you might enter it to put yourself in the presence of more people. Keep your eyes on their hands. If they come at you again, that's when you decide whether to strike—knees, elbows, heel to the shin, you name it (we'll get to this). And if anyone's around, say something direct: "They grabbed me and I need space. I need your help."

2. When They Grab You from Behind (Neck, Shirt, or Hijab)

Let's say you used your voice, your hips, your whole body to escape the wrist grab and start moving, toward people or light. You're scanning. You're breathing heavily. You think that maybe, just maybe, it's over. And then you feel a tug from behind. A hand yanks you backward, hard. This time it's the back of your neck, your shirt, or hijab. They're trying to pull you down, drag you back into their control. Whether they're grabbing flesh or fabric, the intent is the same: to restrict your movement.

Step 1: Protect your breath

Your airway is the priority. Immediately drop your chin to your chest. With this movement, you're shielding your trachea behind the harder bones of your chin and collarbones. Can't get your chin down because your hijab is pulled tight? Turn your chin into your shoulder. This shortens your neck and adds protection. If the hijab is choking you, grab the fabric at the front of your neck with both hands and pull down and forward to reduce pressure, giving your lungs any inch of space you can. And remember, do not yank forward. If they're yanking back and you're yanking forward, you'll only make the choke tighter.

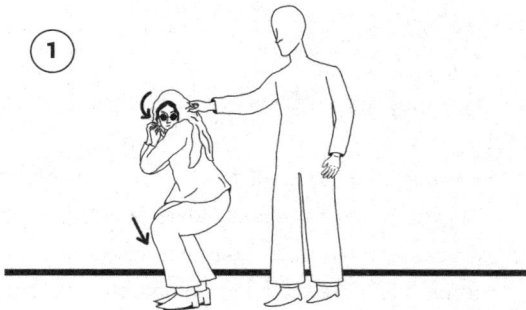

Make sure to exit with the proper stance.
Refer to "When They Grab Your Wrist" exit position.

Step 2: Get into a strong stance and elbow like you mean it

Drop your weight and move your feet shoulder width apart. Then bend both knees and slightly lower your center. Stick your hips back like you're squatting. This makes it harder for them to lift or drag you because you're in a stronger stance.

Trap the arm or hand that's grabbing you: Grab it and pin it to your shoulder, collarbone, wherever it landed. You don't need to rip it off yet. You just need to control it. Step your same-side foot slightly behind you; you're setting up a pivot. Turn toward the grabbing side, into their body, not away. As you twist, drive your elbow backward and across your body. You're aiming for ribs, stomach, or face, whatever is easy for you to reach.

Step 3: Create space

When you land, you should land at 180 degrees and facing them. Put your hands up to create distance and protect your face, just as before.

Be ready to use your voice, defend yourself again, strike, or exit, but ideally exit as soon as you can, moving toward people or light if possible.

3. When They Grab You from the Front

You've turned around and caught your breath. You're now facing them again, and then they grab you from the front. It happens fast. One minute you're regaining control, and the next they're clutching your shirt, scarf, or shoulders. Your instinct might be to yank away. And while that reaction is valid, there's a better way: Swing up to the sky to break free.

Step 1: Ground yourself

Get into a light fight stance. You start by stepping your dominant foot slightly behind the other. Bend the knee on your nondominant leg and keep your dominant leg straight. It doesn't need to be a dramatic step, just enough to give you a wider base. You want to feel rooted, like a tree. By lowering your center of gravity, you make it harder for the attacker to pull or push you and easier for you to generate the power you'll need to get free.

Step 2: Swing up and break the grip

Now let your arms drop down in front of you, palms facing your own thighs. This should feel natural, almost relaxed, like you're gathering your energy. Then, in one powerful motion, swing your arms upward through the space between your body and theirs, aiming straight up through the center of their grip. Use the strength of your whole body, not just your arms. Push up with your legs, let your hips rise slightly, and exhale as your arms fly toward the sky. You are not tugging away or twisting; you are lifting up. Reach your arms all the way over your head, using the full strength of your core, and then swing them back down to your thighs.

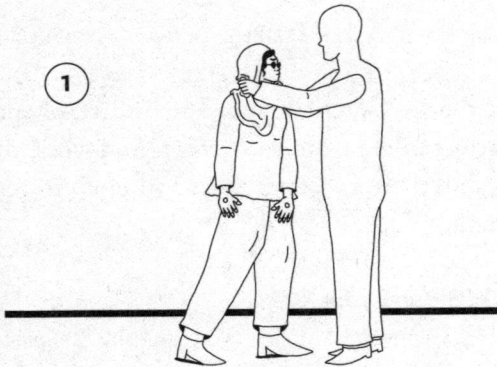

That upward motion, powered by your whole body, is what makes the hold break.

Step 3: Set the boundary with your body and your voice

As soon as your arms are free, don't drop them. This is your moment to hold the boundary you just fought for. Bring your hands down into a strong, clear defensive position, palms out, elbows bent, like you're holding two invisible shields in front of your chest. Your feet are firm, your stance is strong, and now your voice joins your body. Say it loud, say it clear: "Back up." "Don't touch me."

As soon as you can, exit with the strategy I described earlier.

4. When They Swing, Don't Let It Land

You've just broken free from a front grab. You swung your arms up like you were hurling the moment into the sky. Sometimes, even after you've broken the grip and drawn the boundary, the person keeps coming. Their grip didn't work, so now they are trying to strike at you. This is where blocks are really important.

Before you block: Position yourself like you're ready (because you are)

Before any block, your stance is your foundation. Chin slightly tucked, hands up in front of your face, palms facing each other or outward. Elbows are close to your ribs. This is your natural guard: It keeps your most vital zones covered (head, chest, centerline) and lets you move quickly in any direction. It's a typical fighting stance.

Blocks

Elbow block: Your face's line of defense

Let's say things are up close and personal, someone's too far into your space, and they're coming in hot with a punch or an elbow to your jaw. From your guard position, tighten your arm so that your fist is near your opposite shoulder, almost like you're hugging yourself. Your elbow comes up, with your palm at the back of your neck to block the strike. Keep your eyes on the perpetrator as you swing up and back with the other arm. The movement is compact, tight, and protective. You're using the thickest, strongest part of your arm, your elbow, to intercept the strike. This block works best in tight quarters. It's a shield. If a punch is coming in too fast for a full arm block or your attacker is already close, this move keeps your head and neck protected while you figure out your next step.

Wind block: Protection from a straight strike

First bring your blocking open palm down and your elbow of that same arm up like the top of a triangle. You

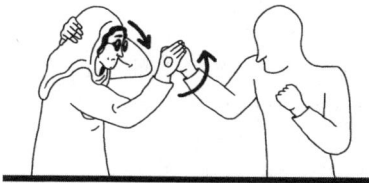

Elbow block

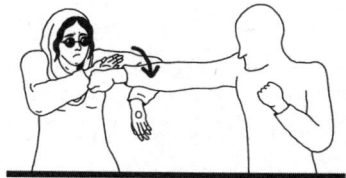

Wind block

Center block (outside)

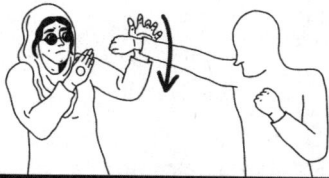

Center block (inside)

Low block

block with your forearm while you're stepping into a strong stance. Your dominant foot steps back, while your nondominant leg stays in front with a slight bend at the knee. As you block, step your front leg forward, to lean in for extra force. The nonblocking hand stays up with your palm open to guard your face and core.

Center block (also called an inside or outside block): Guard the centerline

This is your go-to for straight punches, like a jab aimed at your chest, gut, or face. The goal is not to absorb the punch but to redirect it away from your center. From your guard position, use your forearm to sweep across your body, turning your palm slightly outward. You can also reverse the direction of this movement and sweep your arm across your body outward toward your shoulder to block "outside" (vs. "inside"). Think "wax on / wax off" from *The Karate Kid*. You're pushing the punch off course, usually toward the attacker's outside shoulder. Your arm moves in a curved motion, not a hard block. You're protecting the entire centerline, your sternum, ribs, throat, and belly, with one swift redirect.

Low block: Guard the gut

Now, imagine someone's going for your midsection or lower. Maybe it's a punch to the stomach. That's when you use a low block. Drop your weight slightly by bending your knees more. Then extend one arm downward at an angle, sweeping it across your lower body. Your palm faces out, and your arm is firm. The goal is to deflect the incoming strike away from your body, not absorb it directly. You're still keeping your other hand high, guarding your face, because people often throw high-low combos.

The aftermath: Reset, counter, or exit

The block isn't the end of the story; it's the opening. Once you've deflected the hit, don't freeze. You either reset your guard where both palms are up to protect your face or move your body to escape the danger zone. Your job is to create that tiny window of opportunity to exit.

5. When You're Down

Let's talk about one of the worst-case scenarios. You did everything you could—deescalated, blocked, redirected, tried to exit—but now you've been shoved, tripped, or dragged down. Your back hits the concrete, or the carpet, or the dirt, and before you can catch your breath, someone's on top of you. Maybe they've straddled your torso in what we call a "mount": knees pinning you down, hands maybe flying or pinning you to the ground, trying to overwhelm you with weight and force. This is the moment most people fear: when you're on the ground and the other person is on top of you. But even from your back, even under pressure, your body still belongs to you. And your body is still powerful. Let's walk through exactly what to do.

Step 1: Protect what matters first

If you can, before you do anything else, protect your most vital zones: your face, neck, and ribs. Immediately bring your arms up in front of your face in a tight elbow block: forearms vertical, fists near your temples, elbows tucked in tight to your sides. This position does two things at once: It shields your face from incoming punches and braces your ribs against body blows. Tuck your chin deep into your chest to protect your throat. If you're wearing hijab, pulling your chin down also helps keep the fabric from becoming a tool they can use to control or choke you.

Step 2: Bridge and curve: Use your whole body

First, plant your feet firmly on the ground. Then push your hips up. Not just a little nudge; I mean a full, powerful thrust like you're trying to launch them off. This "bridge" forces their weight to shift, even if just for a moment. Now, while their balance is rocked, curve: Twist your torso to one side, like you're rolling over. Think of it like scooping them off you with your hips. Use the momentum of your twist to throw their center of gravity off. And remember: Don't just roll like you're flopping over. Bridge first, then curve. Use your full power, including feet and hands, to throw them off you.

Step 3: Create space, then get up

Once you've thrown their weight off (or even just enough to shift them), it's time to make space. Shove with your hands,

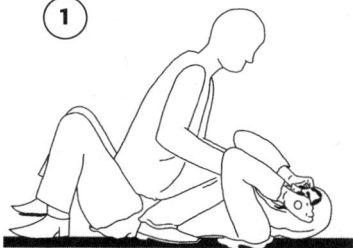

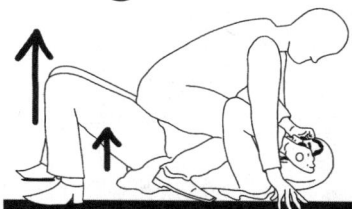

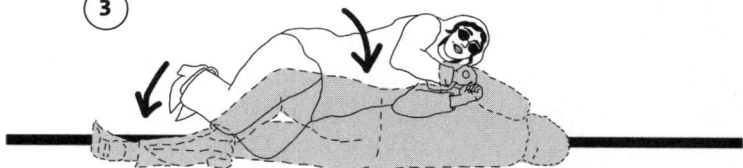

kick with your legs, elbow them if they're close — do what it takes to get a sliver of distance. The moment you've got even a few inches of breathing room, use your legs to push them away. Once they're off you, roll to your side, protect your head, and then use your hands and feet to stand up smart, eyes on them, ready to run or fight if needed.

I KNOW THIS is a lot to take in. I also know that so much of this is highly dependent on this situation that you're in. Maybe you're reading this with wide eyes, thinking, *How on earth am I supposed to remember all of this if something actually happens?* That's fair. Because in the heat of the moment, when your heart's racing and your brain is foggy with adrenaline, you're not going to pause and flip through a mental index of techniques from Rana's book you read one night on the couch. That's not how self-defense works. But you know what does work? Practice. Not once or twice, not perfectly, just consistently.

Because what you're building isn't just knowledge; it's muscle memory. That deep, instinctive knowing in your body that kicks in before your brain catches up. That kind of automatic response comes from repetition, from trying and failing and trying again. So here's what I encourage: Find a training partner (or two) and start practicing (you can even find my training videos online). In my classes, this isn't some scary, rigid process. It's sweaty and awkward, fluid, and kind of hilarious sometimes. It's also deeply healing. Because moving your body in this way, not just to survive but to feel powerful again, taps into something healing. Remember that even with years and years of practice, every technique should be applied based on the specific context you are in. There is always a possibility of escalation, even if you applied the techniques exactly as I described above. You do your best to be as prepared as possible and respond where you can with the most information. No technique is 100 percent guaranteed to prevent escalation, especially when you combine it with the fragility of male ego. Even though self-defense is one of the most effective tools to keep us safe, in addition to self-defense we need real cultural and political change.

Practicing self-defense isn't just about physical safety. It's about emotional safety too. Which means being intentional and trauma-informed in how you train. Always start with consent. Ask your training partner what they're okay with, when they need to pause. Go slow. Make room for the person in front of you, their fears, their lived experience, their limits. Not everyone is ready to practice a choke defense on day one. Some people need to watch first. Some people may need to stop midway through and breathe. Keep your movements controlled. Pull your power back when you're training with someone new. If you're practicing grabs or more intense techniques, check in constantly and create a signal that will indicate when to pause or stop. It'll feel awkward at first. You might giggle. You might mess up. That's fine. That's part of learning. Like any new skill, whether it's yoga, painting, or biking, you start clumsy and slowly find your rhythm.

But I promise you: Nothing is more powerful than witnessing someone discover what their body is capable of. I've seen a woman who is five foot one, barely over a hundred pounds, launch a three-hundred-pound person clean off her. So get on the mat and practice with people you trust.

STRIKE BACK!

ALL RIGHT, WE'VE arrived at the part of the book that most folks think self-defense is all about: The strikes. The kicks. The punches. The moments where you channel every ounce of your strength into one (or twenty) clean move(s). But before we get into how to use them, let's talk about *when* to use them and what the law says about it. Because as much as I want you to own your power, I also want you to be smart, prepared, and protected on every level.

If you're in a situation where your safety is under threat, of course, your priority is to defend yourself with everything you've got. In the United States, where I'm based and where I do most of my teaching, self-defense law generally allows a person to use force to protect themselves, but it's not without conditions. So I recommend: Know your rights by looking up the self-defense laws in your area. Across the United

States, self-defense laws vary by state, but most of them boil down to three main things: immediacy of threat, proportionality of force, and whether you're expected to retreat or allowed to stand your ground.

Immediacy of threat means the danger has to be happening right now. You can't act out of revenge. You can't swing on someone for what they did two days ago. That part is hard, especially for survivors who've lived with fear for a long time, because sometimes the threat doesn't feel like a single moment. But the law says the harm has to be imminent. So if someone raises their fist, corners you, grabs you, that's immediate.

Proportionality of force is about matching the energy. You're allowed to defend yourself, but the force you use has to be considered "reasonable." If someone shoves you, and you pull out a knife and stab with full force, that could be seen as excessive. At the same time, what is truly "reasonable" is complicated, especially when there's a power imbalance. If you're someone physically smaller and the person attacking you is way stronger or has a history of hurting you, you might need to act fast and use a nearby object to get them off you.

In duty-to-retreat states, the law says that if you can safely get away without using force, that's what you should do. For example, if someone's yelling at you in a parking lot but you have a clear exit, the court might expect you to take it instead of throwing hands. In stand-your-ground states, you're allowed to defend yourself on the spot, no obligation to run. If you're in a park, on a sidewalk, or wherever you legally have a right to be and someone threatens you, you can act to protect yourself then and there. That's your right. Then there's the castle doctrine, which kicks in when you're at home. If someone breaks into your space and threatens you, many states say you have the right to defend yourself, even with deadly force, without having to try to flee. Your home is your safe zone. You shouldn't have to run from it.

As with proportionality and imminence, the freedom to actually live by stand-your-ground, castle-doctrine, and duty-to-retreat laws is far from equal. These laws don't operate in a vacuum. They're filtered through systems already shaped by racism, gender bias, and the category of individuals whom society sees as deserving of protection. For example, a powerful and heartbreaking example of this is the case of Marissa Alexander, a Black woman in Jacksonville, Florida. In 2010, after she had separated from her abusive husband, he showed up at her home and threatened her. Fearing for her life, Marissa fired a warning shot into the ceiling. No one was hurt. But she was arrested and charged with three counts of aggravated assault with a deadly weapon.

Now, Florida is a stand-your-ground state. You'd think the law, which was famously used to justify George Zimmerman's killing of Trayvon Martin in 2012, would be on her side here. But it wasn't. Prosecutors argued that Marissa had other options: She could have left, even though she was in her own home, even though her husband had a documented history of abuse. The court ruled that the stand-your-ground law didn't apply to her, and in 2012 she was sentenced to twenty years in prison. It took years of community organizing, led by Black women, to finally secure her release. Marissa served three years behind bars and two more under house arrest, all for an act of self-defense that harmed no one. Her story makes one thing painfully clear: Who gets to "stand their ground" and whom safety laws apply to in America are still shaped by race, gender, and power. Black women defending themselves from intimate partner violence are often punished instead of protected, a reality that underscores just how uneven the playing field is when it comes to so-called justice.

There is so much work to be done to ensure that self-defense law, as it's written *and* as it's applied, is protective and just when it comes to survivors of violence, especially domestic violence. According to a study conducted by Stanford Law School's Criminal Justice Center, there are over twelve thousand women in jail in the United States because of homicide charges. Today, there is not enough research to know what percentage of these women were defending themselves. But a *New York Times* article titled "Who Gets to Kill in Self-Defense?" highlights a landmark study by the National Commission on the Causes and Prevention of Violence, which "recognized that women are more likely than men to be defending themselves when committing homicide," incorporating data from as far back as 1969. A 2024 study titled "Fatal Peril: Unheard Stories from the IPV-to-Prison Pipeline" surveyed 649 women incarcerated in California prisons for murder or manslaughter. Of 134 who were in prison for the deaths of their partners, 110 had experienced extreme domestic abuse during the year prior to their conviction, 74 percent had experienced intimate partner violence (IPV), and about 66.4 percent of respondents who had experienced IPV "were in extreme danger of being killed by their partner the year before the offense."

Research on this topic is new and limited, but what we do know is that self-defense law still does not fully protect survivors of gender-based violence. I hope it never comes down to your life or the law, but if it does, I recommend you choose your life every time. If your life depends on it, you should fight, fight, fight.

Where to Strike

So many of us have been taught to doubt our own strength. To believe that unless we're big, loud, or powerful-looking, we can't fight back. That belief is not just wrong, it's dangerous. I see it in almost every workshop I teach: When I ask participants to strike, to yell, to hold their ground, many hesitate. I get it. I've felt it too. I'm a five-foot-one, 130-pound woman, and for a long time, even with a black belt, I didn't fully believe what my body could do. But I've used technique and leverage to get someone nearly three times my size off me. Because it's not just about size. It's about knowing how to use your body, knowing where to strike, and trusting your muscle memory. Every body has power, especially when you know how to target your attacker's weak points.

Weak points are the self-defense cheat codes of the human body — the spots no amount of gym time, protein shakes, or posturing can protect. When it's time to defend yourself, these are your power zones.

Point in the body	Explanation
Eyes	The eyes are a high-impact target and hard to protect. A quick jab or strike there can be painful and disorienting; it can blur vision, blind, and buy you time to escape. Only go for it if you're in serious danger, like being choked or pinned down. It's not pretty, but it works.

Temples	The temple, the spot between your eyebrow and ear, is where four skull bones meet and arteries run. A solid hook punch here can disorient or even knock someone out. Small target, big impact.
Ears	The double ear slap isn't just for movies. The ears control balance, so cupping your hands and slamming both sides creates air pressure that can rupture eardrums and throw off equilibrium. Bonus: Even if you miss, you're likely to hit the jaw or temple.
Nose	Ever been accidentally smacked in the nose? Instant tears, stinging pain, blurred vision. That's why an upward palm strike or elbow across the bridge can stun or break it. Don't strike straight in—aim for an angle.
Throat	The throat is prime real estate for breathing. A swift punch or chop here can block airflow and stop someone in their tracks. Use this only if you're in serious danger—it's that effective.
Jaw	The jaw is like a shock conductor for the skull. A quick upward strike with the heel of your palm or a tight punch can rattle their whole system. This is why fighters wear mouthguards.

Solar Plexus	Nestled above the belly, this nerve bundle is a reset button for the body. A straight punch here knocks the wind out fast. Way better than going for the stomach, because there's less padding and more nerves.
Groin	No matter the body, this area is packed with nerves. A sharp knee to the groin causes instant pain and shock and often drops an attacker on the spot. It's direct and effective.
Knees	The knees are fragile and crucial for movement. A forceful kick, especially to the side, can buckle them, stop the attacker's mobility, or take the attacker down entirely. Use it to make space and escape. (My favorite!)

I always say, if you remember nothing else from my class, remember the weak points. Burn them into your memory. Because in the middle of fear, adrenaline, and chaos you might forget fancy moves or specific sequences. But if you remember to aim for the eyes, nose, throat, jaw, ears, solar plexus, groin, or knees, you're already ahead. You don't need to be the strongest person in the room. You just need to know where to hit and believe that you can.

If you move through the world with a disability or chronic

pain, or you have limited mobility, and/or you're an elder, like many of the aunties and uncles I've worked with, your self-defense practice will be your own, and that's totally okay. Every body has the right to safety, and every body can practice self-defense in ways that honor its strengths and its realities. The goal isn't to mimic someone else's movements; it's to find what works with your body and build from there. For some people that means striking with your elbows instead of your legs. For others, that might mean using a cane or chair not only for support but also as a tool for blocking or creating distance. If your grip is limited or your hands tremble, your voice might be your strongest tool, able to draw attention and create space. Self-defense is never one-size-fits-all, but every body carries power and every body has ways of accessing that power.

How to Strike

What I teach are simple, powerful, modified strikes that protect you first — things like knee strikes, elbow strikes, and palm strikes — because they're safer on your joints, easier to learn, and incredibly effective when you need them. These are techniques you can use whether you're standing, seated, or just doing your best to stay balanced. I've taught them to aunties in community centers, to people in wheelchairs, and to folks with chronic pain or limited mobility, and they work. Striking is about knowing what parts of your body can generate power and how to use that power when it counts. You don't need to be a fighter. You just need to know what's possible with the body you already have.

Knee Strike

The knee strike is hands down one of the most powerful self-defense moves you can use in a close-range situation, and it's often overlooked in favor of flashy kicks. But kicks require distance and balance, and they leave you vulnerable to being grabbed and taken down. A knee strike, on the other hand, is meant for that up-close moment, when someone's grabbed you, pulled you in, or won't back off. It's quick, it's forceful, and it targets some of the most sensitive areas of the body. You can aim for the groin—a strike there can

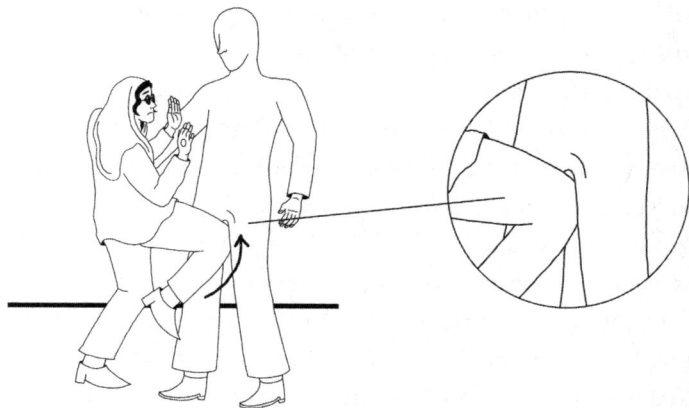

drop someone twice your size — or the lower abdomen or thigh. You're not using your kneecap here but instead are striking with the lower part of your thigh, and you're powering it from your hips. If you've got the chance, with two hands grab one of the attacker's shoulders or clothing and pull them into the strike, as that extra momentum makes all the difference. Make sure you don't bump heads as you're bringing them in close. Create as much distance as possible once you have ensured that the perpetrator is impacted.

Palm Strike

Punching might look cool in movies, but in real life when punches are done incorrectly, it can leave you with a broken hand. That's why I always teach the palm strike instead. It's safer, more powerful than you'd think, and a lot more accessible, especially if you're not a trained fighter and need something that works in the heat of the moment. For the palm strike, start in a grounded stance. Your dominant leg steps slightly back, straight and solid. Your front leg is bent, knees soft, weight centered. You want to feel like you could move in any direction at any time. Your power isn't coming from just your arm; it's coming from your core. Open your hand and strike with the heel of your palm, the sturdy part above your wrist. Keep your fingers loose to avoid injury. Aim to drive your hand through the target, not just tap it. Rotate your hips and pivot your back foot as you strike. That's what generates your real power. Or as Shakira once wisely said, "Hips don't lie." Your hips are everything when it comes to striking, so use them. You can also strike with your nondominant hand instead, if you need to (the opposite of the illustration below), and still bring power to your technique by slightly pushing with full force forward. Aim your palm at the nose (causes sharp pain, blurred vision, and usually tears that cloud vision) or at the chin or jaw (can throw off someone's balance, create whiplash, and give you the few seconds you need). If your grip is limited or your hands aren't your strongest tool, shift to an elbow strike (discussed next), compact, fierce, and perfect for close range. A hard elbow to the ribs, or a sharp jolt forward with your chair into someone's shin? Very effective. If you use a cane, use it to jab at the groin or the solar plexus, or to sweep a leg out from under the attacker.

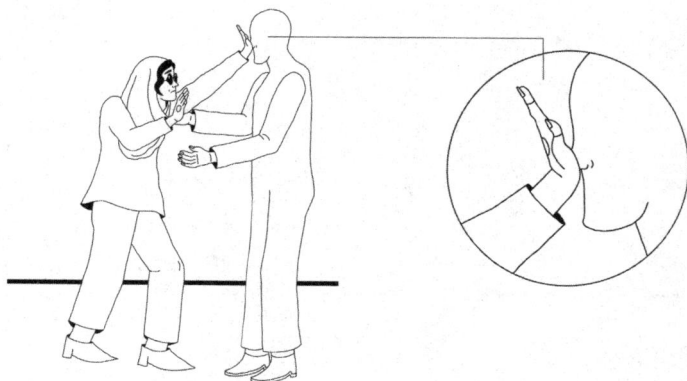

Elbow Strike

Elbows are one of your most underestimated tools: They're sharp, strong, and made for the close-up moments—when someone's in your space, grabbing you, pinning you, pressing in. If someone's directly in front of you or off to the side, draw your elbow back like you're about to nudge someone off a crowded train. Then twist from your hips and drive that elbow in. The power shouldn't come from your shoulder alone; you want your torso and hips behind it. Your whole body is throwing the elbow. Now, targets: The chin or the nose? It doesn't take much to throw off someone's vision or balance. The throat or side of the neck? That can disrupt their ability to breathe for a moment, enough time for you to move. The ribs or solar plexus? Hit them there and you might knock the wind right out of them.

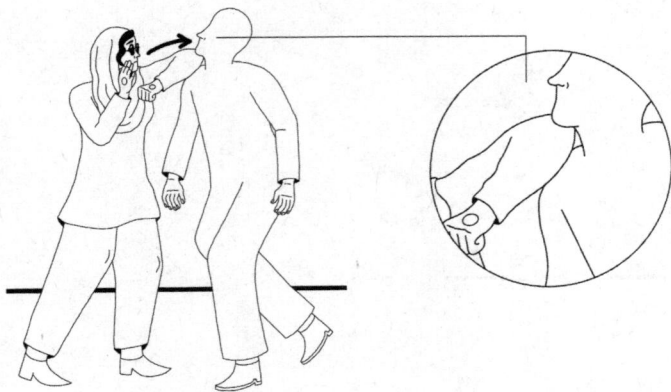

Low Kick

It's quick, it's efficient, and it keeps you grounded. You're using your body in a smart way to create pain, distance, and time, all things you need to get to safety. My personal favorite target? The knee. When you strike it with precision, you can take even the biggest, loudest attacker down a notch. Here's how it works: Instead of swinging your leg around like you're auditioning for a kung fu film, think of it like a sharp stomp forward. Raise your knee slightly and extend your foot straight out, directing your energy right into their knee, shin, or thigh. No fancy spin, just a powerful thrust. Your hips generate the force, and your foot delivers it. Depending on your position and flexibility, you can strike with the ball of your foot, your heel, or even the side of your shoe. Now, where should you aim? The knee is a top choice.

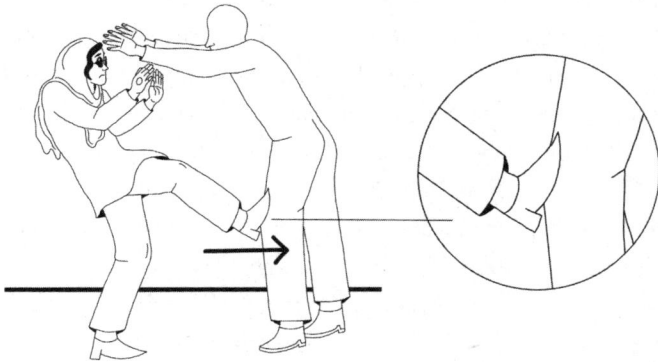

It's fragile. And if you're close enough and their stance is open, the inner thigh is also fair game. It's sensitive and can knock their footing out from under them.

THE MORE YOU practice your strikes, the more they become a part of your muscle memory — not just something you know how to do, but something your body remembers how to do, something it calls on before your brain can even catch up. When you're scared, when your adrenaline spikes, when you don't have time to think, your body doesn't need to remember a list of steps. It just needs to move. Practicing gives your body the permission and the power to respond without hesitation.

At a recent three-week self-defense course I taught in Queensbridge, right near my home in Queens, one participant came up to me after class and shared something. One night, on her way home, a man followed her to the entrance of her building. At first she used her voice, tried to deescalate, tried to keep things calm. But when he reached for her and touched her, something in her snapped into place. She raised her arm and delivered a palm strike straight to his nose.

"He didn't think I had it in me," she told me, still a little surprised herself. But she did. And that one strike bought her the space she needed to run, to escape, to survive. She didn't freeze. She moved. And this, to me, is the point. We don't train because we want to fight. We train because we deserve the right to choose how we respond, with clarity, with control, with whatever strength we've got.

Power doesn't come in a specific shape. It doesn't need six-pack abs or a black belt. It lives in all kinds of bodies, including bodies that are small, soft, aging, disabled, transitioning, recovering, surviving. So when you picture a powerful body now, I hope you can start with your own. I hope you see your body, exactly as it is today, and recognize that it holds power. You don't need every option. You just need the one that works for you, and you need to know it well enough that your body can call on it when it needs it most.

Expect the Unexpected

I WROTE MUCH of this book in Alexandria, Egypt, my parents' home city. Alexandria is very car-centric. While there are sidewalks in some places, the street system operates in ways that make only a chaotic kind of sense. Pedestrians, horse carriages, trucks, ambulances, bikes, mopeds, and cars share a four-lane highway. To cross the four-lane highway with a roundabout in the middle by our house is less of a science than an art, a potentially fatal sport. I try to employ different techniques every time I cross this highway, watching the people around me, and somehow I do not get hit. I've always been the annoying American cousin asking: "Is there any rule to crossing?" "What if we get hit?" "What if someone stops out of nowhere?" Yet much as I've asked about how to cross an Alexandrian street, the answers are all "It depends," "It's about the moment," or just an eye roll and a laugh (at me, not at the street system).

Whenever I teach self-defense, there's always that

moment right after we've practiced a new move when someone raises their hand and hits me with a "But what if . . . ?" And then comes the real stuff: "What if he's taller than me?" "What if I freeze?" "What if I'm carrying a baby?" "What if I'm wearing heels?" These questions are never random. They're coming from people's lived experiences, from fear and memory and the deep need to feel like we'll know what to do when it matters. I always do my best to answer. But more often than not, my response starts with the same two words: It depends. I know it's not the tidy answer anyone wants, but it's the truth. Self-defense isn't a list of exact steps you follow, like baking instructions. It's more like crossing the four-lane highway by my parents' house in Alexandria: no signs, no crosswalks, just chaos. There's no real science to it. You look around, you read the moment, you move when it feels right, and somehow you get across. That's what this chapter is: a little chaos, a lot of "it depends," and the instincts we build to meet the moment when it comes. Like crossing that highway, self-defense isn't always about clear-cut rules; it's about reading the moment, being as prepared as possible, knowing there's uncertainty, and moving anyway. One way we prepare for that uncertainty is by building a safety bag: a small practical set of tools that travels with you when the chaos comes and you need something to reach for.

WHAT'S IN YOUR SAFETY BAG?

ONE OF THE most meaningful things I've done is help survivors build their exit plans. Survivors have come to me in all stages of readiness. Some know they need to leave now. Others are quietly preparing for a moment they hope never comes but are staying ready just in case. My space becomes this safe little war room: a whiteboard, tissues, tea, and a blank piece of paper where we start to imagine what freedom could look like. I start by asking, "What's in your safety bag?" And no, this is not like the trendy "what's in my bag" with lip gloss and AirPods (although I love these too). I mean the real deal: the things that will help keep you alive, safe, and grounded when the unthinkable happens.

YOUR EVERYDAY SAFETY BAG

Even if you're not going somewhere where you expect danger or a sudden need to escape, it's a good idea to think about what safety tools you carry with you in your daily life. This can include:

- **A fully charged phone.** Always. Plus a portable charger if possible. If your phone is your lifeline, it can't die on you. Make sure tracking, across your apps, is disabled.
- **Emergency contacts written down.** Don't just save them in your phone! Write them somewhere physical, in case your phone is not available.

- ▸ **A self-defense tool that feels accessible to you:** Tools like pepper spray, a whistle, or a safety alarm can help you create distance, draw attention, and buy time to escape in public situations. Make sure to be aware of local laws for purchasing and carrying pepper spray.
- ▸ **Copy of (or actual) ID and other important documents:** Your ID, insurance card, immigration paperwork (if relevant), passport, and driver's license. If you have children, pack copies of theirs too.
- ▸ **A flashlight.** Tactical flashlights can be blinding in a pinch, and they're also useful for navigating dark areas safely.
- ▸ **Cash.** Keep a small amount of emergency cash hidden on you or in your bag, just enough for a cab, train, or emergency stop.
- ▸ **Medication.** If you have any regular prescriptions, always carry a day or two's supply when you leave the house, just in case.

THE GOAL IS to start thinking: *What helps me feel prepared? What do I need to feel safe in my everyday world?*

THE FREEDOM KIT

If you are in an unsafe home situation, or supporting someone who is, this bag is different. This is your escape bag, your freedom kit, the thing you grab when it's time to go and you don't know if you're coming back. It's not always possible to pack everything, and that is okay. Here's what goes in it:

- **Everything in your everyday safety bag.**
- **Additional important documents.** Bank account info, medical records, legal documents. Copies are okay if it's not safe to keep the originals here.
- **Additional cash and a nontraceable debit or prepaid card.** Put $50–100 here if you can manage it. Enough to cover transportation or emergency expenses.
- **First-aid kit.** Even a basic one, with Band-Aids, wipes, and pain relief, can be essential in a crisis.
- **Basic toiletries and clothes.** Something clean and comfortable to wear, a toothbrush, deodorant.
- **List of shelters and emergency contacts.** Written down. Printed out. Not just in your phone.
- **Spare phone and charger.** Even a cheap prepaid phone can be a lifeline.
- **Comfort item.** Something small that brings you calm in the moment of crisis.

FROM PEPPER SPRAY TO PANIC ALARMS: WHAT'S ALLOWED?

ON JANUARY 15, 2022, Michelle Go, a forty-year-old Asian American woman, was on her way to work. Simon Martial pushed her in front of a moving train, and Michelle was killed. On January 23, 2022, I gathered with thousands of New Yorkers in Times Square to honor Michelle's life and legacy and stand firmly against anti-Asian violence. Michelle was deeply loved by her coworkers, her family, and the people she spent hours volunteering with. She was clearly a caring, loving, and kind person, and her story was tragic.

Around this time, there was an uptick in pepper spray being handed out across the city through grassroots groups trying to equip community members with resources to stay safe. At Malikah, we have engaged in a fierce debate about whether we should start to hand out pepper spray as well. We've always had the philosophy that our body is the most powerful tool and that introducing pepper spray to our community was introducing a weapon. But ultimately, we did decide to offer pepper spray under the condition that we would ensure our members were effectively trained to use it. I think it's important to be aware of the options, in case you find yourself in one of these contexts.

Pepper spray is that tiny little canister that lives at the bottom of your bag. I'll never forget this woman in one of my Harlem workshops. She walked in wearing a gorgeous hot pink trench coat, sat down, lifted the mini pepper spray attached to her keychain, and said, "I brought my girl." We all laughed. But then she asked, "But... do I actually know how to use her?" It's a real question. Some of us carry these things without ever actually testing them out. When the moment hits, though, and your adrenaline is spiking, fumbling through your purse is not the move. So let's talk through it.

First: Get to Know Your Girl

Before you ever need it, practice. I mean it, practice. Get a dummy can or go outside when the weather is appropriate (please, not in your living room or in a crowded area) and just try spraying it. Figure out the range. How does it unlock? Where's the nozzle? Is it stiff? Does it dribble or spray like a hose? You want it to feel familiar, like second nature, because you won't have time to read the label when a situation is escalated.

Second: Store It Smart

Keep it somewhere accessible, where your hand naturally goes: in your coat pocket, on your keychain, or clipped inside your bag (not buried under your makeup pouch and eighty-seven loose receipts). And if you've got kids around, make sure it's accessible to you, not them. It's not a toy. It's a tool.

Third: Pull It Out Confidently

Extend your arm, away from your face (yes, people forget this). Aim for the eyes and nose, the softest, most sensitive targets. Spray in short, controlled bursts; don't hold it down like you're watering plants. Then create distance and get out of there.

Fourth: Don't Forget the Fine Print

Pepper spray laws vary by state, so make sure it's legal where you live and whether you need a permit to carry it.

Fifth: If the Wind Turns on You

It happens: You accidentally spray yourself, or someone grabs the pepper spray and sprays you. If that burn hits you, hold your breath and close your eyes immediately. If you can, cover your face with a scarf or sleeve. Remove contaminated clothing and isolate these contaminated items in a sealed plastic bag. Wash them in cold water with detergent. Don't rub your eyes. Flush your face with cool water for fifteen minutes. Rinse your eyes with saline solution and your hands with non-oil-based soap. When you can, take a cold shower while keeping your eyes shut as much as possible, as hot water can increase the burning sensation. If you can't breathe, if you experience swelling, or if the burning doesn't stop, seek medical attention.

A FEW MONTHS ago, a Malikah member named Cindy pulled me aside after class. She's a nurse and had just finished a late shift at Elmhurst Hospital Center. On her walk home from the train, she noticed someone behind her. At first she tried to shake it off, telling herself it was probably nothing. But every time she turned a corner, he turned too. Her gut told her something was wrong. Cindy is someone who, like so many of us, freezes in moments of fear. She told me, "Even when I want to scream or speak, it's like my throat closes up. Nothing comes out." That's real. Remember, this is a natural nervous system response.

Luckily, Cindy had her personal safety alarm clipped to the strap of her tote, just like we practiced in class. When the man got too close, closer than anyone should be, she pulled the pin. The alarm shrieked through the block. The man was shaken and backed off, and someone nearby turned to look. The sound alone shifted the moment, and she made it home safe. That's what a personal alarm can do. It gives you a way to take action, even if your voice disappears. It breaks the silence, draws attention, and disrupts the threat. If you're going to carry a personal alarm, here's what matters: Keep it visible and accessible, make sure it works by testing the batteries regularly so it's ready when you need it, and trust your instincts.

Another underrated tool is a tactical flashlight. Not the giant ones used for camping, but small, high-lumen flashlights that fit in your pocket or bag. When aimed directly at someone's eyes, they can cause temporary blindness or disorientation, giving you the few seconds you need to exit the situation. Some flashlights even have a strobe function, which amplifies the effect and adds confusion. To use a tactical flashlight effectively, keep it accessible, shine it directly into the eyes of someone approaching you aggressively, and use the strobe if your model has it (it disorients and buys you time); if needed, you can strike with the end of the flashlight to create space and get away.

I often get the question "Should I carry a knife?" Here's the truth: It's complicated. Knives escalate risk quickly. Once a blade is out, the danger—physical, legal, and emotional—multiplies. If you choose to carry a blade: (1) Be clear on your local laws; carrying certain kinds of knives is not legal everywhere. (2) Get trained. Don't carry something you don't fully understand how to use. (3) Know that once a weapon enters a situation, everything changes and there's a potential for escalation. Someone can easily grab a weapon from you and use it against you.

That's why I often recommend tools like alarms, flashlights, and pepper spray first. In the context of self-defense, weapons should only be used when they are helpful to deescalate and give you time, space, and options, especially in moments when your body is just trying to survive, and only if you're very well trained in using them. It's about listening to your gut, using what you've got, and making it home safely.

OVER THE PAST six chapters, I've shared stories, tips, research, moves, and statistics. Now, take a moment to absorb it all. These chapters are here for you to revisit whenever you need, serving as a practical resource for both your own safety and the safety of those around you. Use them as your guide. Keep in mind that self-defense is a lifelong practice; continuously building your muscle memory, refining your skills, and staying committed to your safety and the safety of people around you will ensure you're always prepared when it matters most. Remember, safety isn't only about the moment of danger. Once you're out, we still face the realities of financial limits, systemic barriers, and structural violence. That's the next fight.

Secure the Bag, Secure Your Safety

MUCH AS I wish it were otherwise, there is no safety without a just economy. Not for survivors. Self-defense cannot be separated from the material conditions that shape our lives: housing, wages, food, healthcare, childcare. I've seen this firsthand at Malikah, when neighbors line up for our food distributions or mutual aid and our Astoria Halal Fridge is emptied within minutes of it being restocked because paychecks run out before the month does. Or when a survivor escaping violence comes through our doors with nothing but her children and the clothes on her back, trying to figure out how she can start over. In those moments, it's painfully clear: There is no self-defense without economic security. That's why it's important for us to be aware of the economic tools that are also essential for self-defense. This chapter is about how we can build more economic power for ourselves so that we can make choices about our safety from a place of power. Then we protect not only ourselves but also the people who depend on us.

I sit with survivors who are trying to find a way out — out

of abusive relationships, out of dangerous housing conditions—and the thing that always comes up is money. When survivors have financial independence, they can make choices that protect them. They can leave. They can stay gone. They can feed their kids. They can access therapy. They can stop answering the calls. Without it, they're stuck, trapped in situations that become more dangerous the longer they stay. Physical safety is deeply tied to economic safety. The world likes to treat them as separate, but they never have been. I've seen that truth play out again and again in my neighborhood, in refugee camps, in courtrooms, in apartments with the lights cut off. Money shapes power. And power is the difference between surviving and slipping through the cracks.

One afternoon I sit across from Salma. She is on the gray couch in front of me. I can't see her eyes, but I can hear the exhaustion in her voice. She speaks in loops, almost as if she is remembering the story while telling it: "He's a good man. We never argued. I don't know what happened." But then the story shifts: "He kicked me out. Took the kids. I've been in this motel. I have nothing." She has access to only one bank account, funded by family back in Algeria so she could survive here. Twenty years in this country. Twenty years by his side. And now she's in a custody battle with no lawyer, no phone, no home, and not a dollar to her name. She watches from the motel window just to catch a glimpse of her children. She hasn't been able to see them; not yet.

When she tells me her husband is a good man, I don't challenge her right away. I wait. I let the story unfold. Then I gently say something in my very American Egyptian Arabic. She laughs at my accent. And just like that, for a second she remembers who she is. Not just what she's lost.

Salma is not alone. Most of the survivors we meet don't expect to leave their abuser knowing they'll have nowhere to sleep that night. They stay because they can't afford to leave. Because they don't have work permits. Because their English isn't strong enough. Because the jobs they do get don't pay enough to live. Because their partners never filed the immigration paperwork. And the world blames them for staying, instead of asking why safety costs so much. Her husband never thought she'd leave. Why would he? Economic dependency is power. He could take more and more from her, and she was expected to hold it all. But she broke the mold. She left even though it was hard, so we helped her apply for mutual aid and we got her a phone. We're helping her find work. But it takes time.

And it's not just one class of people. That's another myth. One night, after a long day, I was locking up the Malikah space when I got an email. Just one line: "Is this Rana? I need help. I have no place to go tonight." I almost didn't see it. I was heading to a coffee shop with a group of aunties, people who had stayed late after the workshop to share ideas and stories. I showed them the message. They insisted on coming with me. We piled into their car, blasting Egyptian *mahragan* music, tossing around theories about what the message could mean.

When we pulled up, the woman we met didn't match what they had expected. She was young, wearing a pencil skirt and sweater vest, clearly a professional, and was dragging two huge IKEA bags behind her. At first glance she looked like she had money. Some of the aunties were confused. "She says she has no place to go, but what if this is a scam? What if she's not really in trouble?" They whispered their doubts in Arabic. But then she looked up. Her face was bruised. Her eyes were swollen from crying. And just like that, everything shifted. Their skepticism melted into compassion. They opened their arms to her the way they always do, fully, without hesitation. They booked her a motel. Offered her food. Asked if she needed a place to stay. Prayed for her. I never got her full name. But for weeks we stayed in touch while she navigated the unforgiving housing system in New York. She was a young professional. She worked full-time but had no savings. Some nights, when she was too ashamed to ask for help again, she slept on a park bench. She refused to go to a shelter because she didn't feel safe enough.

It took time, but eventually she got back on her feet.

This is what I've learned doing this work: Safety isn't just about knowing how to throw a punch. It's about rent money. It's about job security. It's about being able to say no because you have the option. And most survivors, unfortunately, don't.

How do we break out of this? Just like I wish I never had to teach a self-defense class, I also wish we lived in a different economic system, and I work toward that as an organizer. Survivors of violence face disproportionate levels of economic disenfranchisement, higher poverty rates, greater job loss, higher rates of sex trafficking, widespread economic abuse, and increased risks of homelessness. Shouldn't we live in a world where survivors wouldn't need to worry about housing because everyone is guaranteed a place to sleep, because housing is a human right? We need better policies and an economy that is not extractive. We need equal pay for equal work, compensation for unpaid labor, real family leave, universal childcare, and policies addressing discrimination and harassment. True economic safety for women will come from these (and many more) structural changes.

But in the meantime, what we can do is strengthen our own financial wellness. The four economic principles of safety listed here are at least a starting place, a kind of financial self-defense toolkit, which I'll elaborate on through the rest of this chapter:

1. **Develop a skill.** Skills are more than talents that we have; they can become our bargaining power. If you're reading this and thinking, *I don't have a skill,* I promise you do. What are you naturally inclined to do? What's something that you actually enjoy doing? Maybe you're the one in your family who organizes

everything. Maybe you do hair, translate for neighbors, cook for your community, or make art. Start there. At Malikah, we've worked with survivors who turned skills like henna, home cooking, or sewing into a steady side income. But developing a skill means more than just doing the work; it means learning how to price it, how to talk about it, how to protect your time and labor. This skill allows you to make and hold your own resources to decrease dependency on others. Find a community that helps you build not just the skill but also a pathway to income. Look into free online courses, local cooperatives, or economic justice organizations. This is about decreasing your economic dependency and increasing your economic safety.

2. **Join or start a savings circle.** In self-defense, you don't fight alone. The same is true for money. Rotating savings groups have helped millions of low-income people build resilience. But beyond numbers, savings circles are about trust. In a world where formal banks can deny us credit, charge overdraft fees, or make us feel small, savings circles remind us that we are each other's safety net. Start small. Gather five to ten trusted people. Set an amount you can all give monthly. Rotate who receives the pot. Talk openly about financial goals. Use a notebook or a shared spreadsheet to track. In our community,

savings circles have paid for immigration lawyers, flights, rent deposits, even emergency surgery. When one of us is in crisis, it helps to know someone else can get the next month's round. When savings are difficult to maintain and living paycheck to paycheck is the norm, a savings circle is a low-lift, minimal-income way to have some sort of safety net.

3. **Spend hyperlocally.** Awareness in self-defense is about knowing your environment, who is around you, what is available. The same applies to money. According to a 2021 study from the Institute for Local Self-Reliance, $68 of every $100 spent at a local business stays in the community, compared to just $43 when spent at a chain. But beyond numbers, local spending is about building a culture of interdependence. When you buy a meal from your neighbor's catering hustle, you're feeding her children. When you pay the teen down the block to fix your laptop, you're building a relationship. Create a shared directory of local businesses run by folks in your neighborhood. Ask your community spaces, mosques, churches, and mutual aid hubs to hire them. This helps extend that safety economy beyond yourself.

4. **Give what you can as locally as you can.** Giving doesn't have to be huge to matter. Create a giving

habit. Set a monthly transfer to a mutual aid fund. Or if you know someone who is part of your healing space who might need support, check in to see if starting a fund for them would be helpful. Keep $5 in your wallet to hand to someone on the street. Offer childcare to a parent in your community trying to get to a job interview. Giving builds our collective muscle for mutual care, and one day that safety net might catch you too.

DEVELOP A SKILL

AT MALIKAH, MOST of the women who walk through our doors are looking for one thing: a job. For them, it's a way forward, a way to stop depending on someone who hurts them, a way to stop being invisible in a country that has made survival feel conditional. They don't always use the word "job." Sometimes they say, "I want to do something." Or "I'm tired of asking for help." Or "I don't want to go back." And sometimes they say nothing at all. They just show up quietly, sitting with a kind of hunger that isn't always about food. It's about worth.

Maybe it's the auntie who's been doing henna since she was twelve in her town but never charged for it. Maybe it's the mom who speaks four languages and has been translating at school meetings, clinics, and courtrooms for neighbors for years. Maybe it's the girl who does braids after school to buy her own lunch, or the one who knows how to manage an Excel sheet better than the office manager who hired her. Yet, over and over again, they'll say, "I don't have a skill." They say it because no one has ever told them otherwise. Because we're trained that only certain kinds of labor count. That if it's not in English, if it's not digital, if it's not in an office or on LinkedIn, it doesn't matter. But the truth is, what you know can save you. Not in some metaphorical, lofty way, but in a real, rent-paying, boundary-setting, confidence-building kind of way.

Imagine a woman whom we'll call Samira. She's recently left a partner who abused her. She has two children. She's staying with her mean cousin in a one-bedroom apartment. No income. No papers. She's in survival mode. When she comes to a healing circle, she sits in the back. She doesn't say much. But when the group shares snacks after the session, Samira brings a small tray of cookies. Homemade, perfectly shaped, wrapped in wax paper and ribbon. She insists they're "nothing." But everyone eats them. People ask if she sells them. She laughs it off. What if she did? What if someone sat down with her and said, "Actually, this is something. Let's talk about what it could become"? That moment, a moment of naming a skill, isn't just about entrepreneurship. It's about safety. Because if Samira can make $300 a week selling cookies, through her mosque, the school, her neighbors, or even just at local events, that's $300 she doesn't have to ask for. That's $300 she can use to buy her kids' school supplies, pay for a MetroCard, or save toward her own place. That's $300 closer to independence.

You probably already have something. A talent, craft, hobby, or skill. A way of caring or creating that could become a real, powerful source of income and independence. You're also probably reading this while cooking dinner, holding a crying baby, or in between shifts. You are managing so much—home, family, school, work, healing, community— and the idea of "starting something new" might just feel like another thing to do. I get it. This guide isn't about adding more to your plate. It's about helping you find the value in what's already there, what you already know how to do, what you've already been doing for free, what's already in your hands. And it's about figuring out how to get paid for it on your terms so that you have your own income.

START WHERE YOU ARE

YOU DON'T NEED to quit your job, launch a brand, or open an Etsy store tomorrow. Ask yourself:

- ▸ What do people always ask me to do?
- ▸ What would I *enjoy* doing if I could get paid for it?

Examples:

- ▸ "People come to me to braid their daughter's hair."
- ▸ "I'm the one who organizes everything at school."
- ▸ "I help folks with paperwork in Arabic and English."

You're probably already doing the work. Let's name it.

Try It Small — Like, Really Small

You don't need to start a "business." You can just *try something.* One order. One gig. One ask.

Maybe you tell your cousin, "I can braid your daughter's hair for $25." Or you say at the mosque, "I'm making trays of *basbousa* this Friday if anyone wants to buy." Even just testing the waters builds confidence and opens doors.

Make Time that Works for You

You're busy. So set a *realistic goal* that matches your capacity:

- ▸ One paid project per month
- ▸ $50 extra income this month
- ▸ One hour per week to work on your skill

You don't need to hustle every day. You need to build something sustainable that fits your life, not overwhelms it.

Respect *Your* Time, Even If Others Don't (Yet)

You might feel awkward at first, charging for something

you've always done for free. But your time matters. Try saying:

- ▸ "I'd love to help. I charge $30 for that."
- ▸ "I can offer a sliding scale if needed, but I don't do it for free anymore."
- ▸ "This is my business now. I'm proud of it."

You're not being selfish. You're setting boundaries. And boundaries *are* safety.

If you spend two hours making a tray of *sambusas*, it costs you $12 in ingredients, and you want to pay yourself $15 an hour: $12 + (2 × $15) = $42 → you charge $45.

If You Can, Do This with People You Trust

Everything is easier in community. Grab a friend. Start a little skill-share circle. Text each other goals. Check in. Celebrate every small win.

SAVING IS A SAFETY PLAN

MOST OF US are tired. We're working multiple jobs, taking care of kids, trying to keep up with rising rent, grocery prices that somehow just doubled, and bills that never stop coming. In America today—in the *world* today—survival itself feels like a full-time job. So when people say "You should be saving," it can feel like a slap in the face. How are we supposed to save when there's barely enough? When most Americans, nearly two-thirds, can't afford even a $1,000 emergency expense? So saving together might be the only way some of us can save at all.

Growing up, I saw saving principles in practice through a concept called *gam 'iya*. Some know it as a *susu*, a *tanda*, or a rotating credit circle. But the heart of it is the same everywhere: We are the bank. We are the safety net. We are the backup plan. A *gam 'iya* is a traditional savings circle, commonly practiced in Egypt, particularly among women. In this informal financial arrangement, a community of eager savers, typically friends or family, comes together and agrees to contribute a set amount of money on a regular basis, such as weekly or monthly. Each member takes turns receiving the pooled amount, usually in a rotating order.

For example, if ten women are in a *gam 'iya*, each might contribute $100 each month. In the first month, one person receives the full $1,000; in the second month, another person gets the $1,000; and so on, until everyone has had their turn to receive the lump sum. Every year when I was young, I witnessed my mom participate in a *gam 'iya* when she wanted to save up some money, whether to take a flight to Egypt or to pay for an Arabic teaching certification program. It is pretty genius because you can commit as little or as much as you want based on a mutual agreement with friends. My mom and her friends would know when someone had sudden medical costs they needed to cover right away, and sometimes they would shift the order of the rotation in order to address that financial crisis.

As I've mentioned, this practice isn't just common in Egypt. In Nigeria it's called an *esusu*; in India it's a *chit* fund; in the Philippines it's a *paluwagan*; and in Jamaica it's a box. If you can't save on your own, start a *gam 'iya* and save in community. Build your bank on existing relationships of trust, center empathy in the practice, and use it to work toward a goal.

So How Does It Work?

It's simple, and you don't need a fancy app, a financial advisor, or a stack of spreadsheets to make it happen. What makes this model special is that it is fully based on trust. There is no formal contract, only relationships. In ways, it pries open one of our most closed-off and taboo topics, personal finance, and creates a sense of collective finance. You start by gathering a group, maybe five or ten folks you trust. You could include friends from work, sisters from the mosque, neighbors, cousins, or that one reliable auntie who always knows when you're going through it before you even say a word. You choose people who understand the grind. People who know what it means to stretch a dollar, who won't flake when it gets hard. The kind of people who already show up for you in small ways. Together, you decide how much each person can commit to contributing every month. Maybe it's $25. Maybe it's $100. Maybe it's just $10 to start. You choose something that feels doable, something that stretches you a little but doesn't break you.

Each month one person receives the full pot. The next month it goes to someone else. You rotate until everyone's had their round. And then you keep going. Because even after you've received your round, someone else is depending on you to keep that commitment. The circle holds because people stay in it. And here's where the magic is: When someone's in crisis — when the car breaks down, or the landlord decides to raise the rent out of nowhere, or a family emergency back home demands an expensive plane ticket — the group can rearrange. Maybe you move her round up. Maybe someone covers her contribution that month.

You can keep track however you want. Some folks use a simple notebook. Others use a group chat, a Google spreadsheet, or a printed-out chart taped to the fridge. It doesn't need to be complicated; it just needs to be clear. And it helps to say your goals out loud: "I'm saving to send my mom money." "I need to cover legal fees." "I want a little cushion in case I have to leave my job." And if you're thinking, *I don't know if I have people who'd do this with me*, take a second. Look around. Whom do you turn to when things are tight? Who helped you with childcare last week? Who split groceries with you when your EBT ran out? Whom did you stay with when you broke up with your ex and had to move out? That's your team.

Even a small amount saved, $100 or $200, can give you breathing room in a moment of crisis. It can be the difference between staying in an unsafe situation and getting out. Between feeling stuck and feeling like you have options. Women with access to savings, whether through formal institutions or informal circles like these, are significantly more likely to leave abusive relationships, avoid predatory lenders, and regain control over their lives.

SPEND HYPERLOCALLY

AS I'VE THOUGHT more about what makes us truly safe, I've come to realize that every dollar we spend is not just a transaction but also a reflection of our values. Where we put our money tells the world what we stand for, whether we're supporting systems that harm or those that heal. It's not just about buying things; it's about building something bigger, a safer world, and in our communities. For me, this idea of local economies has been a game-changer. When we spend locally, we're not just supporting a small business; we're also investing in the people around us, our neighbors, our community, our families. And that's what creates a culture of safety. It's not some abstract concept; it's about real people, real businesses, and real economic power. When you start your business, you've sparked a local spending chain that will, inshallah, find its way back to you.

When you spend money in your own neighborhood, with people you know or know of, you're doing more than buying a product or service. You're building a relationship. You're helping someone stay rooted. You're saying: *I see you. I want what you're building to grow.* One of my favorite examples of this is Modify, a modest-clothing shop in Harlem that's now run by a Black West African Muslim woman who took over her father's business. She didn't just keep the doors open; she reimagined it. In a neighborhood that's been hit hard by gentrification, she created a model that's both affordable and community-centered. People can bring in modest clothes they're no longer wearing and swap them for credit and some cash to get something new to them. It's a circular economy model that makes modest fashion accessible, while also keeping clothing out of landfills and building trust in the neighborhood. Places like Modify remind us that small businesses can be more than storefronts. They can be gathering spaces, resources, and even support systems. When we spend our money there, we're investing in more than a product; we're investing in the kind of community we want to live in.

Imagine a community where a woman who owns a local cleaning service might hire another woman from the community to help with childcare, or a local shop owner might provide mentorship to a woman wanting to start her own business. This is the way my neighborhood in Astoria, Queens, operated when I was growing up. *We* created a flexibility, care, and safety economy where people could take care of each other because they knew each other. From Arabic classes taught by Taunte Azza and cleaning services by Taunte Mona to sewing workshops by Taunte Amal and catering by Taunte Maha, we've created opportunities for women to be their own small business owners without massive capital investment up front. Local businesses tend to have more personal connections to the people they serve. In many places, women are disproportionately represented in low-wage, informal, and often exploitative sectors of the economy. When we choose to spend locally, we're less likely to support businesses that exploit workers, particularly women, in unsafe conditions. Many large corporations cut costs by outsourcing labor to low-wage workers, including women, in countries where labor laws are weak or nonexistent. When we prioritize spending with local women-owned businesses, we know that the money is more likely to stay within the community and circulate among people who care about one another.

So How Do We Actually Start Spending More Locally?

It can be small. Maybe you decide to get your hair done by someone in your building instead of the cool salon across the city, or you order food directly from a local family-run restaurant instead of through a delivery app. Maybe you look for a babysitter who lives nearby, or you share a friend's business flyer in your WhatsApp group. Maybe before buying something online, you pause and ask yourself, "Do I know someone offering this already?" Go across the street to the corner store and see if the price isn't too bad there. Then you meet the cashier, and over time, this becomes a safe place to leave a spare set of keys or to duck into if you're feeling unsafe walking home.

These shifts don't have to be huge to make a difference. Spending locally builds trust. It keeps money circulating in the community. And when something unexpected happens, such as an emergency, a job loss, or a health scare, it's often those same relationships that become the first to respond. Not because anyone owes you anything, but because you've already built something together.

If you're not sure where to begin, start by making a short list:

- ▸ Who in my neighborhood is offering services or selling things I usually buy elsewhere?
- ▸ What are three local businesses I want to support this month?
- ▸ How can I share or uplift the work of someone I know?

Local isn't just about geography; it's about relationship. When we spend where our feet are planted, we make our communities more sustainable, more connected, and a little bit economically safer for all of us.

GIVE WHAT YOU CAN

WE'VE TALKED ABOUT developing a skill, saving what you can, and spending locally, but there's one more piece to this puzzle that ties everything together: giving. Even if it's just 1 percent of your income every week, every month, or every year. The act of giving, whether money, time, or resources, might seem small, but over time it builds something so much bigger. It creates a community that's ready to show up for each other when the inevitable happens. It builds safety. And let's be real: None of us can predict when we'll be in need. Life throws curveballs—job losses, health problems, economic crashes—and when a crisis hits, it's not just the individual who suffers; it's the whole community. But if we've been consistently putting into that community, we've already built a safety net to catch us.

I learned this again during the pandemic. When my mom got sick and we were struggling to meet even the most basic needs—groceries, medicine, essentials—it was tough. We couldn't leave the house because of her illness, and we had no way to get what we needed. But what really got us through was the generosity of our community in Queens. Neighbors we didn't even know that well started dropping off bags of groceries at our door, offering meals, and checking in on us. It wasn't just about food; it was about knowing that there were people out there who cared, who saw our struggle and stepped up. It was so beautiful and touching.

That experience stuck with me, and it's part of why I started running a community fridge and food distributions every week since the pandemic. We knew that if we were going through this, there were others in the neighborhood who were struggling too. We've now distributed thousands of meals and grocery items to families in need, thanks to the support of so many in our community. Most of our recipients, you can guess, have been women.

Because here's the thing: We never know when we'll be in need, and that's why giving back is so important. We live in a world where most people are one medical emergency, one job loss, or one crisis away from financial insecurity. In fact, 59 percent of Americans are just one paycheck away from being homeless. If we don't have that safety net, because we never helped create it for others, we can end up lost in a heartless, dysfunctional system. But when we give, we build that safety net. We create a cushion for ourselves and for others, and we make sure that no one is left to struggle alone. This is resistance against a system that keeps people poor and vulnerable. When we give to mutual aid funds, local charities, or community-run initiatives, we are investing in the infrastructure that allows everyone to rise, not just survive, and this is what keeps women safe.

When we have that kind of support, when we know there's a community ready to back us up in times of crisis, we feel safer. We feel empowered. The community becomes a place where we can take risks, make choices that are in our best interest, and find safety. The impact of even a small contribution is amplified when it's consistent. Giving regularly creates a culture of shared responsibility and mutual care. It reminds us that we are all connected and that the well-being of one person is tied to the well-being of all. This is how we build safer, more just, and resilient communities where violence, economic or otherwise, has no place. So, no matter how small, giving makes a huge difference. Whether it's a little bit of money each month or a few hours of time each year, it all adds up. We all deserve to live in a world where our safety and well-being are determined not by how much money we make but by the community we're part of. And if we all put into that community, we create the kind of world where women can thrive, free from violence and full of possibilities.

BUILDING SAFETY MEANS putting what we can into our communities: developing our own skills to create income and options, saving together so no one is left alone in a crisis, spending our money with people we know and trust, and giving, however we can, to support others. Each of these practices is a small but powerful way to push back against isolation and scarcity. Together, they create a mutual aid ecosystem: a network, where safety depends not on luck or income but on community connection.

These strategies, while essential, are still individual- and community-level responses to systemic problems. They help us survive. They buy us time. But they don't undo the structures that keep so many of us vulnerable. Self-defense teaches us to block, strike, and move, but also to look for exits and call for back-up. In the same way, financial skills are powerful tools, but they are not the final fight. If we want real safety, not just for ourselves but for every person, we have to change the systems that create the harm in the first place. That's why the next step for a safer world is to organize.

Build a Safer World Together

AS MUCH AS I love self-defense as a healing and protective tool, it shouldn't be necessary. I'd much rather do martial arts because I'm an athlete and not because I know the reality of violence that shapes the lives of survivors each and every day. We should exist in a world where people can walk down the streets of their communities with restful hearts. We should exist in a world where the walls of our homes bear witness only to what is soft and kind. We should exist in a world where our bodies do not carry the lingering sting of violent hands. We should exist in a world where everyone is safe. We should. We do not. The gap between what the world should be and what it is—that is where community organizing is so essential. Self-defense is not just what we do with our bodies in the moment of danger; it's also how we organize together to confront the systems that make the danger possible. Community organizing is the practice of self-defense on a larger scale, a collective act of resistance and imagination to build a world where we do not need self-defense classes to feel safe, because safety has been secured through just systems. What follows is a guide for understanding political organizing as a form of self-defense, to inspire us to create a safer world.

SYSTEMS-BASED CHANGE IS NECESSARY

WE KNOW THAT we will be safe only if we are economically, socially, emotionally, physically, and politically safe. For all of our fundamental safety needs to be addressed, we have to engage with the systems and structures around us that create conditions of insecurity. For us to be safer, we build our emotional safety, physical safety, financial safety, *and* political safety toolkits. I know this probably sounds a bit lofty, maybe even abstract, until you see how it plays out in real life.

There is a woman who walked into Malikah's purple storefront yesterday. She is undocumented and low-income. Spanish is the only language she speaks. She's confused about why I speak Spanish. Yes, I'm Egyptian, *but* I am from Queens, I tell her. She has a young child on her hip, and she stands up to reiterate a point she's just made. She tells me that she has just come to the United States, escaping war in her country. Now she is fighting a war in her home.

Her name is Lolita. Her partner is the sole financial provider, working multiple jobs to support their family back home and pay their New York City landlord. The jobs are backbreaking and often heartbreaking, too. Lolita and her partner navigate the streets like a minefield. Since they arrived, they have not had the courage to make eye contact with anyone. I explain to her lightly that New Yorkers don't make eye contact, and most of them have trouble affording rent too, so she's fitting right in. She feels sobered by what their life has become and has empathy for why her partner has become more stern, angry, and controlling. He is her first love. Even the way he lashes out makes her feel less alone after a day of isolation on the arduous and never-ending job hunt. But yesterday was different. He beat her the way she'd seen her father beat her mother. That crossed the line for her, and she found her way to us. In a world where the systems and structures are different, Lolita would have options: As a mother, she could easily find long-term permanent housing, free childcare, or a guaranteed basic income. There could be a world where Lolita's husband, as an asylum seeker and survivor of violence, would have access not only to labor protections but also to mental health spaces through community and grassroots healthcare provision. But I have limited options to offer her today. Let's just take her housing circumstance. She is forced to stay in an unsafe home because domestic violence shelters are over capacity, are unsafe, and have robust litmus tests for entry. In the National Network to End Domestic Violence's Annual Domestic Violence Counts Census, New York City providers report that housing and shelter are consistently the most requested yet unmet services. If she does get into a shelter, the respite is temporary (in New York State there is a limit of 180 days on shelter stays). Plus the transition rate from shelter to permanent housing is lower than ever. Between 2019 and 2023, the national average for successful placements from emergency shelters, transitional housing, and similar programs into permanent housing decreased from 40.9 percent to 32.4 percent. Policy needs to change this.

Across the United States, 57 percent of homeless women report domestic violence as the immediate cause of their homelessness. Domestic violence is the leading cause of homelessness for women and children in the United States. Say Lolita does scrape together funds to find an apartment or shared housing opportunity. Will she have the resources to find food? Or will she spend hours in the cold in line at food pantries across the city? Lolita can't work because she doesn't have childcare. She doesn't have childcare because she has no income. Even if she were middle-income, as of 2025 the average cost for full-time, center-based infant care in New York City is very expensive, approximately $10,000 to $20,000 per child. She must rely on her husband's income because she has no work permit due to the immigration backlog for asylum seekers. Even for those whose asylum applications have been approved in the United States, the average wait time for a work permit is 180 days or more, all depending on the service center handling the application. Lolita can find safety in local community organizations, but if she calls the police, she might be deported, her husband might be detained, and both of them could be subjected to extreme levels of police violence and risk being separated from their child. All outcomes she does not want, obviously. Lolita loves her husband and wants to find space for mediation, therapy, and his rehabilitation. Even if this infrastructure did exist, it would be way too expensive in dollars and in time (he works more than fourteen hours a day). She understands how the violence of their circumstances, including his workplace and the trauma of their journey, has resulted in his extreme anger. She doesn't forgive him yet, but she doesn't see how jail or deportation would help her and her child. They have no options.

I think by now you understand that this is not exclusively a New York story. Today, survivors of domestic violence across the world, just like Lolita, have very limited options. For her baseline safety from physical abuse, Lolita would need housing, childcare, mental health care, and an effective approach to addressing the root of the violence.

Mona is a teenager I met in Za'atari, a refugee camp in Jordan and one of the largest refugee camps in the world, established in 2012 and now home to approximately eighty thousand Syrian refugees. Mona was thirteen years old when she arrived at the camp with her parents, fleeing the brutal war in Syria. By the time I arrived to teach self-defense through a gendered violence prevention initiative, she had been there for four years. I met her when she was seventeen, and we spent two months in a self-defense class together, learning strikes and grappling techniques and talking about her experience. Mona's family, like most refugees, was still struggling to adjust to life in the camp. Even basic necessities — access to water, electricity, and even quality food — were hard to come by.

But Mona wasn't just facing the trauma of war and leaving her home and the uncertainty of her future. She also suffered gendered violence in the camp. An officer started to target her. His abuse started subtly at first, a sexual glance and licking of his lips here, a flirty passing comment there, but soon it escalated and became physical. Mona was terrified. She could feel the soldier's gaze on her every time she stepped outside her family's tent to go to school, which was a sweltering walk away. Her body, slight and young, became his object of aggression, and yet she had nowhere to go, no one to turn to. When she described this story to me for the first time, during a break in a self-defense class, she looked pale and numb.

One day, as he reached out to grab her, Mona ran. She ran and ran and ran until she found refuge behind a small trinket shop where a tin-foil-covered shed provided some protection from the scorching heat of the desert sun. She huddled in the small shadow, pressing her back against the walls. But time dragged on. The sun came up, and it set again. She sat there, with no water, her face turning a deep cherry red from the sun, her clothes damp with her tears. She didn't know how long she could keep hiding, and she was scared. When the shop owner finally came to open the store, he found her, exhausted, dehydrated, with the marks of the sun and her trauma on her body. Her face revealed her devastation, and her parents had to confront the reality of their daughter's pain. But even then, they had no solutions for what had happened to her. As refugees, under the control of camp authorities, they felt they had no choices. If they spoke up, they would likely experience more violence. So Mona's parents, like many parents, decided that the only way to keep their daughter safe was to keep her close, restricting her movements.

After many screaming matches between her mother and father, it was decided: School, once an important part of Mona's life and a core value for her parents, felt less important than her safety. That night her father approached her gently. He couldn't even make eye contact as he softly apologized to her for having to pull her out of school. He couldn't protect his own daughter. The aid workers in the camp blamed it on culture.

Mona is not alone. Research on women in Za'atari shows a pattern of sexual and gender violence. Forty-one percent of the women and girls in Za'atari report rarely, or never, leaving their shelter because of feelings of insecurity. In general, survivors of sexual and gender-based violence are more likely to report incidents to other family members than to service providers or the police. But as we know, violence is not only perpetrated by strangers. Fifty percent of the survivors seeking support services are survivors of domestic violence. Syrian women have reported that their husbands are under immense stress and that this increases physical and psychological violence against them and against children within the home. Incidents of sexual and gender-based violence are most often reported to have been perpetrated by male relatives (husbands, uncles, and brothers).

As the other girls in the self-defense class listened to Mona tell her story, they were pissed. Why should Mona be the one to sacrifice so much when she had done nothing wrong? How was this fair? Now she'd lost everything. Others chimed in to share about what they saw and experienced.

Mona should not have to live in fear because she was forced to flee a war that already claimed so much of her childhood. Like Lolita, she deserves dignity. Like Lolita, she deserves safety. And like Lolita, she should have options. The officer who harassed her should have been immediately held accountable; she and her parents should not have had to be so afraid of retaliation. Mona should have space to process her experience and regain her power. In fact, she shouldn't be in a refugee camp at all, where she is isolated in a dangerous limbo of uncertainty and could be ejected from the country at any moment.

Then there is Sofia. I met Sofia during a self-defense class I taught on a college campus. She was a student, young, hungry, and eager, like so many of the students who show up to a self-defense class like mine. But Sofia wasn't looking for ways to defend herself against street violence or the typical dangers we talk about in class. When Sofia walked into the room for the second class, she was distant. Over time, though, through the classes and conversations, Sofia began to open up and share her story with me.

It started at the beginning of the semester. Sofia, like 26.4 percent of all women in US colleges, is a survivor of campus sexual assault. She had been sexually assaulted by a classmate she trusted, someone she knew from her community of friends. Six out of ten victims of rape and sexual assault know their offender. This was someone she had studied with, played sports with, and built a deep, trusting relationship with. At first she didn't know what to do. She felt ashamed, confused, and isolated. The assault felt like it had erased her sense of safety, not just on campus but in her entire world. She wondered what her classmates and parents would ask. She wondered if it was her fault. She *had* said no. She *had* established her boundaries. Still, she felt deep shame for having been (as she saw it) naïve. She stewed over questions in her head that she anticipated she would be asked if she reported the assault. Could she have done something different? What had she been wearing? Had she been intoxicated? Why had she let him come so close? As she played her answers in her head, she felt small. It wasn't just about what happened to her physically. It was also about what she felt had been taken from her: her sense of safety.

For a while, Sofia did not report. Unsurprising, since more than 90 percent of sexual assaults on college campuses go unreported. But eventually, because she felt so isolated and unsafe in the spaces they shared together (including one of her classes), Sofia went to the campus administration. She thought that, surely, at a university, there would be measures in place to help her, to protect her, to hold him accountable.

When she first went to the campus Title IX office to report the assault, she was met with warmth and an intention to support. But then she was forced to recount her story over and over again. The paperwork was long, the process unclear. She was told that it could take months before a formal investigation would even begin, and in the meantime, her rapist was still walking around campus, still attending classes with her, still in the same social circles. She was told there was just nothing they could do, though; there was a process in place and it had to be followed.

She asked about the possibility of changing her classes or getting some distance from her attacker, but the response was always the same: "It's complicated." So Sofia was left to sit in class, day after day, knowing that the person who had assaulted her was just a few feet away. She had no choice but to continue seeing him, hearing his voice, living in constant fear that he would approach her, speak to her, or worse. The support she was promised felt empty and inaccessible. She couldn't find the resources she needed to make sense of what had happened, nor could she get the help she needed to feel safe on her own. All she wanted was space, distance from the person who had hurt her, and a way to heal. Instead, the system left her to make her own way. It was clear that at least in part, his status as an athlete and someone from a wealthy family shielded him.

The systems that create and perpetuate gendered violence don't confine themselves to refugee camps, low-income women, or immigrants, although data make it clear that marginalized communities are disproportionately targeted and harmed. Gendered violence manifests across class and social spaces. It reaches into elite universities, middle- and upper-class suburban homes, corporate boardrooms, Hollywood film sets, and halls of political power. No amount of money, status, or education confers immunity from the structures that enable and excuse abuse.

Privilege changes how violence is experienced and concealed. In corporate environments, for example, cultures of silence and complicity are often camouflaged by polished statements about diversity, equity, and inclusion. Perpe-trators use wealth, reputation, and institutional power as shields. High-profile scandals in politics, entertainment, and higher education have long shown us how abusers are pro-tected by the very systems that claim to keep us safe. The normalization runs so deep that we live in a country where a US president has been found liable for sexual abuse.

Those without privilege are left with even fewer resources, avenues for reporting, or power to challenge perpetrators. Refugee camps, immigrant communities, and low-income spaces often experience gendered violence within their imme-diate social structures that is compounded by the systems of oppression. In addition, research, cultural narrative, and pol-icies (sometimes backed and amplified by other women, often with privilege) facilitate the normalization of gender-based violence. Here, the threat of retaliation, deportation, or losing basic safety and sustenance can create insurmountable barri-ers for those trying to seek justice or protection. Sofia wasn't just dealing with the trauma of the assault. She couldn't focus in class. She couldn't study. The emotional toll was drain-ing. Her grades began to slip. She began to withdraw from friends and activities. Every part of her life was affected by the fact that she had nowhere to turn for true safety. She took a semester off, but when she came back she was still reeling from the pain of the experience. I could see it in her eyes that day. He was still on campus. His life hadn't changed at all.

She was too afraid to tell her friends, as they all moved within the same social circles. In a world in which the systems were designed with our safety in mind, Sofia would have had her class schedule adjusted, a no-contact order in place, and counseling readily available. Her attacker would have been removed from her environment, and she would have been provided with clear, easy-to-understand resources to support her through the process. Instead, her options were limited to a broken system that dragged its feet while she was left to deal with the aftermath. Sofia's story is one of many in which survivors of gendered violence on campus are forced to navigate an indifferent and ineffective system while their physical and mental health, their friendships, and their precious, often exorbitantly expensive educations suffer. Like Lolita and Mona, Sofia needs a system that prioritizes her safety, not her rapist's reputation. She needs an approach to addressing violence that doesn't leave her constantly battling the institutions meant to protect her.

I am confronted with these realities almost every week. *Wallahi*, it keeps me up at night. Sometimes we can help. I will pick you up in the middle of the night and find you a hotel room. We'll start a mutual aid fundraiser and find you a job. We'll refer you to another organization that has more resources, and we will follow up on your case. I will go with you to your court hearing and translate from Arabic to English. We will develop your safety plan, help you pack your bags, and help you furnish your new apartment through a mix of Amazon wish lists and mutual aid. We sit and listen and brainstorm options together. This is why we exist. Our work is important. But it is, very transparently, never enough. This is why we are committed to creating change, block by block, in our community in Astoria, Queens. I understand that a different world should exist, and that Lolita, Mona, and Sofia should be safe. To be safe, we need to organize.

But let's be real about what that means. Organizing isn't just showing up to a protest or posting a graphic. Organizing is about building power and community. It's about creating the conditions for real, lasting change, the kind that reshapes policies, shifts budgets, and makes sure that people like Lolita, Mona, and Sofia don't fall through the cracks. It's about fighting for protections and resources that actually change the material conditions of our lives and make us safer. That kind of work takes structure. It means leadership development, political education, campaign strategy, base building, follow-up, and consistency. It means showing up even when you're tired. It's losing and trying again. It's power in the slowest, most intentional form. And, honestly, it's heavy. Especially when you're just trying to survive.

So yes, we need structural organizing. We need people fighting for legislation, building coalitions, shifting systems. That's a part of the work, and it's essential. Without it, individual acts of self-defense exist in a vacuum. With it, we begin to practice collective self-defense that doesn't just protect us in the moment, but helps us protect each other through generations.

Just like in physical self-defense, collective self-defense is a practice with many strategies. It's a discipline we can learn, repeat, and build together. Here's what that looks like:

1. **Imagine you can win.** Just as you have to believe in your strength to strike, organizing requires imagination. Believing we can build a different kind of world is the start of building that world.

2. **Scan your surroundings.** Awareness comes first. Know your block, your school, your community. Pay attention to the policies, budgets, and power structures that shape safety outcomes for yourself and your community. Then find your stance. Your stance is your values. What are you fighting for and who are you fighting with? Root yourself in a safety that is about justice, dignity, and collective care.

3. **Use your voice.** In self-defense, shouting "stop" is your power. In organizing, testimonies, campaigns, and public presence disrupt violence and demand change—that is your power. Then redirect the force. In martial arts, you turn the attacker's force against them. In organizing, transform state violence into demands for justice.

4. **Protect others.** Organizing does not happen alone. Build coalitions for safety, show up for others, and defend those who are most vulnerable, just like in bystander intervention.

5. **Practice builds power.** Muscle memory comes from consistency, and so does political power, in the form of regular meetings, canvasses, protests, calls, and votes. Each small act builds collective power.

6. **Find your joy.** In self-defense, we don't just train to fight; we also train to breathe, heal, and shake off the fear that makes us freeze. The same is true in organizing. Joy isn't a distraction from the movement; it's what keeps us in it. Celebration, dance, prayer, and rest are essential parts of creating safety. They remind us of what we're fighting for and give us the strength to keep on going.

IMAGINING YOU CAN WIN

ONCE WE UNDERSTAND how the systems in place are failing to protect so many of us, it's also important for us to *believe* that a different world is possible — and that we are capable of building it.

What does a safe world look like? Sound like? Feel like? I always ask this at the end of my self-defense classes, but most people struggle to imagine it. We're so accustomed to the world as it is that we stop thinking we can end the violence. But real change requires imagination. It demands that we see past the systems built by those starved of humanity and envision a world where women and girls are truly safe, free from violence in their homes and on the streets. We start with this big vision, and then we break it down. We apply it at the local level, to ourselves and our neighbors and our block.

I think back to the day in early March 2025 when former New York governor Andrew Cuomo oh-so-shamelessly launched his campaign for mayor of New York City. I was pregnant, and it was so cold outside that I couldn't feel my face or my feet or fingers. But somehow I could feel the wetness of my face from the tears rolling down my cheeks. Somehow I could feel the pulsing knot growing in anger at the center of my throat. There were about sixty of us gathered at the corner of a building as union members lined up to enter the room where Cuomo was about to relaunch his entry into politics, less than four years after he was pressured to resign in the wake of findings made about his sexual harassment of women, detailed in a report released by the New York State attorney general. Over a dozen women had come forward to date, despite his retaliation and the danger to their safety, careers, and reputations.

That cold day, a group of us — a collective of women from across the city, from Staten Island to Queens — had gathered to protest his campaign announcement. Some of us approached the podium, standing in front of the press mics, speaking in Spanish or English, our voices trembling in anger. Some of us shared our own stories of sexual violence. We read the depositions, pieces of his accusers' testimony about the way he groped, kissed, and harassed women around him. I was shaking because the words coming out of my mouth felt so disgusting. But I was numbed by the thought of what has become of our city and country and world. I approached the podium, and in my remarks I tried to channel my rage: "If Cuomo returns to power, it will send a dangerous message: That the powerful can get away with anything. That justice is just a word. That survivors don't matter. This is a man who was accused by over a dozen women of sexual harassment, women who risked everything to tell the truth. They described groping, forced kisses, inappropriate comments. They spoke up, knowing how powerful he was." The stakes felt so high for the city I love so much. And yet we've already elected a convicted felon and sexual abuser to the highest office in the nation. Twice.

What a time to be writing this book, to be emphasizing the epidemic of gender-based violence. Despite years of organizing, #MeToo, #TimesUp, so many of us finding the courage to stand up and fight back, here we are: visibly in regression. Our tolerance for violence seems impossibly high, and the backlash to our powerful stands in the past few years is taking us back to a culture in which it is perfectly acceptable for the mainstream political class, even in a progressive bastion like New York City, to stand behind a man with this kind of record.

Some good news: At the time I was writing this, Andrew Cuomo had failed to win the Democratic primary. Instead, a beautiful, unruly, deeply rooted coalition of grassroots organizations came together, including people from all walks of life, to push forward a new kind of leadership.

I thought back to that first day of Cuomo's candidacy, when I'd stood outside freezing with other members of the Working Families Party, and said to myself: *We really did it.* We had kept someone who perpetuated violence against women out of the highest office in our city. We'd made space for a different future, against all odds, against the seemingly unshakable structures of power, against all assumptions we might have made based on the status quo we know is all too real in this country.

Let me be real with you: Despite moments of hope, despite the wins, it might feel easy to throw up our hands now. Like, what are we even doing out here, after we thought we'd come so far? It might feel easy to lose hope.

We absolutely cannot.

We can exist in a safer world. I believe that; otherwise I wouldn't work so hard. We don't have to start our work from the top. We don't have to take on the federal government or get in front of the Supreme Court on day one. Oftentimes the most important work is right down the block, right here at our feet.

SCAN YOUR SURROUNDINGS AND FIND YOUR STANCE

I ORGANIZE FOR safety locally. I don't understand what life is like on your block, in your neighborhood, in your community. That's why you hear me talking so much about my beloved Queens, because it's the place I know best. But you are an expert in your place and among your neighbors. While the culture of misogynistic violence is pervasive, the way it shows up and the resources needed to address it are specific to each community. That's why the first principle of organizing as self-defense is to scan your surroundings. Pay attention to the patterns of harm where you are, the policies that shape your daily life, and the assets already in your community.

To organize, you don't need a degree, or to fly to somewhere far away. The people who can use your voice and power are all around you. You see it in the faces of your friends and family. You know it. You feel it. So this movement should be as pervasive and omnipresent as the violence. To borrow from the Argentinian fourth-wave feminist movement that spread across Latin America: *Ni una menos*, not one woman less. We cannot sit idly by as more of us die because of gender-based violence.

Awareness alone is not enough. Plant your feet and find your stance. That means taking seriously the patterns of harm that surround you, refusing to normalize them, and rejecting the silencing of survivors. Those of us who have been impacted by violence know deeply, in our core, how consequential this erasure is. From that stance, we root ourselves with a clarity about what we're fighting for and whom we're fighting with.

Once we reorient ourselves to internalize that gender violence is never acceptable, then we can begin to activate against the systems that uphold and normalize it. For me on that cold March morning, this meant trekking into Manhattan to make sure that the mayor who was going to represent my city in the next term would not be someone with a deeply harmful record of sexual violence. It meant reminding people of what he had done, ensuring that his actions were not normalized and that he, like so many men before him, wouldn't get to fail up. This act was political self-defense, a way of saying that our safety depends not only on ourselves in the moment but also on challenging those in power who perpetuate violence with impunity.

When I work with members of my community who are escaping domestic violence, or as I watch the cost of rent, eggs, and childcare rising alongside the rates of domestic and hate-based violence, I feel overwhelmed too. There's an internal voice that says: *Maybe you should just look away. Maybe you should just keep your head down, go to work, survive the day, and let it go.*

But as my baba often reminds me, *that* is what they want. For us to feel so crushed that we retreat into individualism. That we disconnect from one another. That we forget our power. He'll then offer a *hadith* from the Prophet Muhammad, peace be upon him: *If you can't change something with your hands, then speak out against it. And if you can't speak, then feel it in your heart.* At the very least, it is not normalized inside you.

WHEN I WAS fifteen, I wanted to do something, but I had no idea where to start. I looked around me, scanning my surroundings to find my stance. That's when I remembered something the women in my neighborhood had taught me without even knowing it. They didn't wait for things to change for them; they built their own safety nets. They supported each other in ways that allowed them to thrive despite everything stacked against them. They taught me that real change begins with what you have, right in front of you. So I started there. I thought, *What do I know?* Well, I know karate. I'm a competitive athlete. I know how to defend myself. I know how powerful it is to be in control of my body, to know how to stand up for myself in a world that has often made me feel small and vulnerable. That was my starting point.

And so I began offering those free self-defense classes in the masjid. I knocked on doors, talked to parents, to leaders in the community, and to young women, and eventually thirteen girls from the neighborhood joined my classes. At that point I started to realize that it wasn't just that I knew karate. A five-foot-one hijabi girl teaching self-defense in a basement? People were skeptical at first, but when the girls showed up, we found something deeper than self-defense. With each lesson, we not only learned how to throw punches and defend against attacks; we shared our stories, we laughed, we cried, and we built a sisterhood. We started to understand that safety isn't just about physical defense. By the end of the summer, we were a community, and that made us so much safer. And that's when it hit me: This was only the beginning.

You know all about your own experience, too. You also have a passion or a skill. If you're a survivor of violence who is passionate about writing, those are intersecting perspectives that can have a deeply important impact. You don't need to go get a PhD in the anthropological manifestations of gendered violence to create spaces for change. From organizers and women leaders who have created change before me and around me, I've learned that you need to give yourself credit for what you know and what you believe. Start the change from there.

Identify Issues Specific to Your Community

Before you can work to make a change, you need to understand what you're facing. Reflecting on your own experiences and the community around you will help pinpoint where the real issues lie. Reflect on your personal experiences and observations to identify the specific gender violence issues in your community or environment.

1. What everyday experiences, at home, in public, at work, or online, make me feel unsafe as a result of my gender, identity, or lived experience? *What patterns, behaviors, or systems create or reinforce that feeling?*

2. What conditions or systems make members of my community vulnerable to harm, control, or exploitation? *Think about institutions (like policing, housing, and healthcare) as well as cultural or economic forces.*

3. What forces (social, political, economic, or interpersonal) push people in my community into situations where their safety, dignity, or bodily autonomy is at risk? *What do we tolerate or overlook that enables these harms to continue?*

4. When have I felt deeply safe, supported, and empowered? *What people, practices, values, or environments
   helped create that sense of safety?*

5. What does community safety look like when it's rooted
   in care, justice, and accountability, not punishment or
   surveillance? *What models or strategies could we build
   or strengthen to make that vision real?*

USE YOUR VOICE
AND REDIRECT THE FORCE

IN MARCH 2025 I was asked to be co-emcee for an event
gathered by Nalafem, a pan-African feminist council that
I'm proud to be part of. We had come together to discuss the
ongoing genocide and war in Sudan. For local women, the situation had been especially devastating. The United Nations
reports that sexual violence has become a systematic weapon
of war, and in some areas 50 percent of women and girls have
experienced rape and other forms of abuse. Brutal. This was
not my memory of Sudan. I had been to Sudan for a wedding,
and my memories were of joyful ululation, of generations of
family packed into one house, of the sweet aromas of *bukhoor*
(incense), henna, and slowly cooking meat. The music made
days blur into nights and nights feel like days.

This gathering was very different. The room hosted activists, artists, and scholars and was heavy with the weight of
their stories, stories that had become all too familiar. It was
in this atmosphere that I had the honor of introducing someone whose very existence, whose very work, had defied the
odds and changed the course of history: Leymah Roberta
Gbowee. During my introduction, I paused, took a deep
breath, and said, "It's not every day that you get to listen to
the words of a woman who literally is credited for ending a
civil war in her country." She bowed her head before smiling
at me as she rose to the podium to speak to us as young African feminists. Her story showed me what it really means to
use your voice to protect others around you.

Leymah's name carries a legacy of hope and peace, in
Liberia and around the world. Liberia, much like Sudan, had
been devastated by war from 1989 to 2003. The conflict left
over 250,000 people dead and more than a million displaced.
During that period, sexual violence against women was
rampant, with rape being used as a tool of terror. That day
Leymah reminded us that 70 percent of women in her country experienced sexual violence during the war.

But in the midst of this chaos, Leymah Gbowee emerged
with many other women, not as politicians, not as global
leaders with access to power, but as community organizers, as mothers, and as women who simply couldn't accept
the violence anymore. Leymah, alongside other women,

founded Women of Liberia Mass Action for Peace, a grass-roots movement that sought to end the war from within. They organized sit-ins, peaceful protests, and powerful demonstrations, with one of their most famous tactics being a "sex strike" (Lysistratic nonaction), where women refused to have sex with their husbands until peace was negotiated. Brilliant. These were local, ground-level solutions that only they could come up with. Not even a multimillion-dollar organization with all the academic expertise in the world could understand their perspective and mobilize as power-fully and effectively as they did.

As she stood up to speak, I could feel the room shift. In a way, it felt like she was speaking directly to me, even though I had never experienced war, and I surely didn't feel like I had the power to stop one. She spoke of her childhood in Liberia, a time when community bonds were tight, when neighbors knew each other so well that even if you got into a fight with someone, you'd have their shoulder to lean on in tough times. It reminded me of my own upbringing in New York City: how being poor didn't mean going to bed hun-gry because neighbors would always share, and how fami-lies looked out for one another. As she spoke, I caught the eye of an auntie beside me, wrapped in a thobe from Sudan, who whispered that her experience growing up had been the same.

Leymah spoke about the atrocities of war, about the

rape and violence that women faced in Liberia, about the way survivors had to fight simply for the right to survive, with no space for dreams or hopes for tomorrow. She told us that if you've experienced the trauma of war, you know what it means to simply fight to stay alive, to not think about tomorrow. "Do you know that kind of survival?" she asked us. But despite the fear, despite the overwhelming terror, she and the women who stood with her managed to change the course of their country's future, something that to many had seemed unimaginable. They stood up to soldiers with guns; they pushed through the fear of retaliation; they published peace petitions with very little in their pockets. Even when their neighbors and family laughed at them, they pressed on.

She reminded us that their movement was not one of "international organizations or global leaders." They redirected the force of their pain into organizing, prayer, and public protest, building a movement so powerful it ended a fourteen-year civil war. Women of Liberia Mass Action for Peace, which began in 2003 with just a dozen women, eventually grew to over 2,500 women, both Christian and Muslim. They held daily nonviolent protests and staged sit-ins in highly visible locations like fish markets, churchyards, and government buildings, and during peace negotiations they blocked the exits of the buildings in which the negotiators were working, literally locking the doors and refusing to allow politicians and warlords to leave until they came to an agreement. The result? The pressure led to the signing of the Accra Peace Accord in August 2003, officially ending the war and paving the way for the first African woman elected as head of state, in 2005.

Yet the movement didn't go without criticism. Many dismissed it as naïve, too emotional, too grassroots, too feminine to take seriously in a conflict defined by guns and power. Some called it symbolic or unserious. Others questioned whether ordinary women had any right to demand peace at all. But the members of this movement kept going. They knew that real safety would come from their own courage, their own communities, and their willingness to show up, again and again.

Leymah's words were a rallying cry to all of us: "You need to stay put. We must be in our communities, not in boardrooms, not in international offices, but on the front lines where the real work is being done." She spoke about the importance of local solutions, solutions born out of the lived experiences of those who suffer the most, who understand the depth of the struggle in ways that outsiders simply cannot.

And it's not just in Liberia. From Northern Ireland to Sudan to Colombia, women have been on the front lines of their own communities' battles, advocating for peace during the most violent periods, helping to pave the pathway to safety for hundreds of thousands of people. To organize, to create safety for ourselves and for others, we don't need permission, and we don't need external actors telling us what to do. We start with what we know. We start where we are, and with the power of our own lived experience, we can create the change we seek.

"Men with guns fear the women who make peace," Leymah reminded us, and those in the room nodded, eyes brimming with tears, but hearts filled with renewed hope. In those moments, we realized that change, the real change we were seeking in our everyday lives, wouldn't come from an NGO or a Senate bill. Or at least we didn't need to wait for that. In the end, Leymah's proudest moments, as she said, were not winning the Nobel Peace Prize or achieving global recognition. They were the moments when she walked through Liberia and the people there recognized her as a woman who had helped bring peace to her country. That recognition, that connection to her community, was the ultimate reward. If Leymah could do it in the midst of a civil war, we can protect our communities too. We are the experts of our own lives. Use that expertise.

Identify Your Power Based on What You Know

Once you've pinpointed the challenge, it's time to turn inward and figure out what you bring to the table. What unique skills, perspectives, and experiences can you leverage to make a change? The best activism doesn't come from a place of obligation or pressure; it comes from authenticity and using what you already know to make an impact.

1. What am I naturally good at? *Think beyond your job title. Are you a connector? A deep listener? A creative problem solver? A person who keeps others calm in a crisis?*

2. What brings me joy or energy when I do it? *Sustainable work is rooted in joy. What do you love doing that could be in service of others? What makes you feel most alive?*

3. What lived experiences, skills, or forms of knowledge do I carry that could build safety, whether physical, emotional, spiritual, or economic, for myself and others? *This could be formal knowledge, like training in healthcare or martial arts, or informal but essential knowledge: navigating systems as an immigrant, raising children, surviving harm, finding healing.*

4. How has my background—cultural, spiritual, familial, educational—shaped the way I see and respond to gender-based violence? *What lessons were passed down to you? What silences did you grow up with? What truths*

have you had to unlearn, and what truths have you reclaimed?

PROTECT OTHERS AND PRACTICE

LET THE EFFECTIVE altruists come for me, but maybe we don't need more people trying to "save women over there"; for real, it's giving colonialism. Instead, we need more people consistently building safety, joy, and power right where they are. There is so much harm in framing a certain kind of people as being disempowered or a certain kind of person as being inherently violent. There is so much harm in positioning yourself or a certain group of people as more capable of creating change than others. And there is so much harm in the kind of support that is like a parachute, promising so much but providing it only in small doses that end quickly. It strips us of our agency. In the world of social media activism, it's tempting to think you need to have all the answers or to swoop in quickly as an expert to make a difference. Many of us think change is instant and that it can happen overnight. But as modern-day philosopher Kendrick Lamar says, "Be humble, sit down." Protecting each other starts with humility, recognizing that every community carries its own knowledge, strategies, culture, and leadership. To protect each other is not to rescue; it's to stand alongside, to listen, to amplify, and to act in solidarity. That kind of work requires consistency and relationship-building over time. This means we show up for each other again and again and again.

The truth is, real safety for a community requires grassroots leadership. I'm all about solidarity, amplification, and showing up when it's needed most, as long as the voices of those most impacted are at the center. One of my own organizing experiences started in the fight against police brutality facing Black people in the United States. I believe in building grassroots power right where you are, through relationships we take the time and care to cultivate. That's exactly how I started: with the people I knew. With my mom, my sister, my homies, my dad, my husband. They're all involved. They're all part of this vision to create safety right here in Queens. Through this, I've learned that the most beautiful, loving relationships are the ones tied together through a shared vision of collective safety and liberation. It was me showing up to march and take action over and over again.

Real safety, after all, is the abundance of human connection. It's a world where we feel so safe that there's no barrier to engagement between me and the person I just crossed paths with on the street. Where the possibility of joy and friendship is everywhere. Safety must start with authentic, genuine human connection. My community shows up at the doors of Malikah when they need help because they've been to our block parties, our potlucks, our healing circles, our community markets, or because someone they trust told them this was the place to come.

So I ask you: Who are your people? Protect each other.

When I started at fifteen, the only community I had a real connection with were the girls in my neighborhood. I didn't know what it meant to be a Senegalese immigrant in the Bronx or a Bengali girl in Brooklyn, but I did know how to be a young woman in my own community, and that was enough. The women who raised me, who held their families together with sheer determination and love, had something essential to teach me. They didn't just survive; they built. They created strong networks, shared resources, and provided each other with emotional and financial support. I learned that community is power, and that I could leverage my relationships to create more power.

Finally, about two years ago, after fourteen years of teaching self-defense, I was able to cobble together the resources and find our place on Little Egypt's Steinway Street (one of the hottest spots in Queens—if you know, you know). The storefront used to be a law office and was a grand total of 1,000 square feet, but there were no rats in sight, and it had a long hallway that made our little nook feel safer. A New Yorker's dream. My baba helped me take down the old golden letters that read LAW OFFICE and replace them with white letters that read MALIKAH on a deep purple background. On Google Maps, I created a business listing for the Malikah Safety

Center under the category "self-defense school." Anyone who owns a small business will tell you about what it feels like to look up with blurry tear-filled eyes and see a sign on a storefront with the name of your vision in real life — in my case, on the neighborhood block where I grew up. We made it.

So we had the sign up, and even if there were no mats for classes yet, not even Wi-Fi, people in the neighborhood began learning about the new safety center on the block. In my head, I'd been thinking of the safety center as a place where we were going to teach a couple of self-defense classes a week, facilitate healing circles, offer financial wellness programs, and maybe teach some Muay Thai and kickboxing on the side. But as it turns out, the people know that safety is a much broader concept than that. And my people? Well, they came. One week in, before we even had chairs, we had community: a domestic violence survivor looking for a place to stay, a new mother who needed help filling out a food assistance application, an asylum seeker who was looking for a job, and an auntie who'd had her wages stolen by her employer. Nada, the sweetest Egyptian girl in my neighborhood (now a social worker and a Malikah employee), my mama, and I quickly began to activate the auntie network and community organizers to find solutions for these women. I didn't always realize it while it was happening, but this was community love in action.

To be truthful, at first I resisted. We already had a stated mission and a tag, and these services were way outside of the programming we had planned to offer. We would refer our people out to trusted organizations or resources, but our people would come back to us. We were right in the neighborhood, we spoke Arabic, they knew me. *Okay*, I thought, *we can help just this one time.* I already knew that safety isn't just a physical state. But here in this small office, still barely set up to function, was its physical manifestation. For women in my neighborhood who took a self-defense class with us, safety was being able to escape an abusive relationship at home, or being able to stay in their homes in the face of the rapid gentrification of our Astoria neighborhood. It was having enough food to feed their children. It was having a dignified job. Safety was knowing they would be able to walk down the street and not get harassed for being visibly Muslim. As someone who grew up in this neighborhood, I understood this all too personally. So in between the self-defense classes, housing application forms, and court hearings for domestic violence survivors, I started to think about building long-term safety for the women and girls in Little Egypt.

As the relational organizing expert Marshall Ganz tells us, to build relationships we need to expend the time and energy to listen to others and understand their needs and motivations. It's all about creating trust, and that takes time, consistency, and transparency. Trust is the bedrock of any successful movement. That's why I often envision the role of an organizer as a lifelong commitment to a neighborhood. That relationship eventually can grow beyond the local to include other community groups, always working in coalition. Especially if we hope to never leave a place (or be displaced), we can build more and deeper connections and slowly, authentically grow the circle of people we stand with. Over sixteen years later, I feel that our community's power has grown precisely because we've built from the inside out. We didn't start with grand declarations. We started with presence. With showing up for one another, again and again. And because people know me, because they've seen my consistency, understand my motivations, and have felt my commitment, they trust that I'll show up for them. And they'll show up for me. That mutual trust is the foundation for true solidarity.

When your work is rooted in the people and places you're accountable to, it can stretch outward in integrity. That's how coalition grows—not from saviorism or the desire for visibility, but from shared struggle, deep listening, and relational reciprocity. When we link with others who experience harm in similar ways, through gendered violence, displacement, policing, or economic insecurity, we don't stand above or for them. We stand with them. That is the quiet, steady power that transforms movements: people who are in it not just for a moment, but for each other.

That's the kind of organizing I've tried to build in Queens, with people I know, rooted in consistency, care, and deep accountability. With an intergenerational team, we opened a mutual aid hub in Queens for survivors of gender-based violence. With the influx of asylum seekers in New York City, I launched a mailroom that now serves over a thousand homeless and asylum-seeking neighbors. I created a food distribution program delivering more than fifteen thousand culturally rooted hot meals a year. When people walked through our doors as parents trying to hold down an apartment, we started a cash assistance program, and now we distribute thousands a month in direct relief to help people survive violence, evictions, and the systems that have failed them. And somewhere along the way I earned the nickname "The Mayor of Queens." I say this with deep humility. People call me that not because I hold public office but because they know I'll show up, with groceries, with flyers, with karate pads, with whatever the moment demands.

This is what it means to build power from the ground up: not to speak *for* others, but to build *with* them. And when our roots run deep, when our organizing is grounded in the places and people we love, we can stretch toward others who are fighting their own battles. That's when solidarity becomes real. That's when movements can grow.

I WILL NEVER forget the summer of 2017. It was Ramadan. The fasting days were really long, but because it was a summer Ramadan it meant that in Queens and in every Muslim community across the United States we youth were overjoyed. By June 18, we were in the last and holiest ten days: a feast, hours of worship, post-midnight caffeine runs, and hanging out with your homies. That Saturday I stayed up too, doing laps between our Astoria masjid and Martha's Country Bakery on Ditmars Boulevard for black-with-extra-sugar coffee for several aunties and bags of desserts for everyone else. I woke up the next day groggy and slow, and started scrolling through Facebook.

There was a block of text: "Nabra Hassanen, Hijabi Muslim Girl, Murdered with an Axe Last Night After Prayers in D.C."

No no no no no. My head was spinning and I was in disbelief. I read on: "Official Statement: Nabra Hassanen Murder Must Be Investigated as a Hate-Based Attack."

On June 17, Nabra Hassanen had been praying at a Muslim center in Virginia. She left with her friends to grab something to eat before it was time to fast again. She never made it home. Instead, on that holy Ramadan night, she was hit in the head with a bat and raped. Then her body was dragged a quarter of a mile to be dumped into a nearby pond. I couldn't stop scrolling and I couldn't stop crying. I felt like Nabra could have been anyone I knew.

Almost immediately the police started undermining the real story with the claim that this was "a traffic dispute." No

acknowledgment of the femicide or the underlying Islamophobia in the incident. Angry and heartbroken, I called everyone
I knew in the area around where Nabra had lived and died.
Because of organizing I had done for over a decade nationally,
I had built trust, and after getting approval from her family
(with whom I managed to connect via another neighbor), I
started to mobilize people. By Tuesday we organized vigils
in ten cities across the United States. #JusticeforNabra began
to trend as we reclaimed the story being told to us by police. I
went down to DC and found, in the center of Dupont Circle,
hundreds of people gathered there; tens of thousands more
were gathered in other places across the country, Muslim and
non-Muslim, interfaith, interlocking, fasting.

Signs read WE WILL DEFEND EACH OTHER. In my remarks,
I connected Nabra's death to a broader pattern of dehumanization of Muslim women and girls. I spoke about the
heartbreak of femicides, about the "Muslim ban," and about
the escalating political rhetoric that painted our communities as threats. This wasn't an isolated incident, and it felt
like a profound betrayal to hear so many so-called leaders
speak about it as though it was. In those seventy-two hours,
I barely slept. I was writing strategy and communications
documents, coordinating press, hopping on phone calls
with local organizers, working with our incredibly talented
designer, and taking the train down to DC. But here's the
truth: We couldn't have pulled this off without the people I

already knew, without the relationships we had been building for years. This action didn't come from nowhere. It came
from my friends, mentors, collaborators, and students, people I had trained with, prayed with, learned from, built with.
Folks I'd organized retreats with, facilitated healing spaces
alongside, marched with for Black Lives Matter, and walked
with through hard seasons of life.

It wasn't just the logistics or the strategy that made it
possible; it was the deep trust and shared purpose between
us. This was a mobilization rooted in community. It wasn't
sparked by an institution. It was sparked by us. Because we
knew each other, we could move quickly. We could grieve
together and act together. We showed up for Nabra. We
showed up for each other. We showed up for our shared identity as Muslim women. We showed up to refuse to accept
dehumanization as our fate.

That experience reinforced for me that organizing starts with
the people you know. It starts in living rooms and text threads,
in study circles and school hallways. You can't change things
alone. You have to build, nurture, and rely on your people. We
applied our skills, our knowledge, and our collective power to
take action, and while we didn't get the accountability we hoped
for, the solidarity we built brought a kind of strength, grounding, and closure that comes only from being in community. It
was community that helped me not to fall into indifference, both
regarding whom this work is for and whom I'd do it with.

I'm not saying people are easy. Sometimes it's the people you know, the ones you build with, the ones you love, who break your heart the most. You'll grind for hours and no one will show up. Your voice will go hoarse from chanting. Your shoulders will ache from the zip ties holding your hands behind your back and cutting into the skin of your wrists. Your knees will give out after six hours of standing. You'll be too angry to look anyone in the face as you take the shoelaces out of your sneakers before heading into a tiny cell.

Even after all that, you'll watch violence happen anyway. A woman you've organized with for years will lose her children to an abusive husband. A domestic violence survivor you tried to protect will be detained and deported. Sometimes the betrayal will come from inside your own community: silence when you needed support, judgment when you needed care. You will shout for justice, and it will feel like no one is listening, not even the people you thought would always have your back. But even then, especially then, I remind myself: You can't organize in isolation. You can't fight for a better world alone. You still need your people, messy, complicated, imperfect as they are. Because real community is not about perfection; it's about building safety with each other anyway and sticking together, beyond "cancel culture" and through accountability and community.

So what keeps us going? Imagining the win.

When you are on those streets and people *do* show up,

you will witness the purest bliss of humanity. Elders and young people, arm in arm, singing as one, in a ring of protection around a group of Muslims praying. You will bear witness to what sacrifice our hearts are capable of when you surprise even yourself by pausing and stepping back to grab a stranger who is caught in a cloud of tear gas, risking your own sight. But in that singular moment, your vision is clearer than ever. You will be fed by strangers and you will feed strangers. Everyone is family. Your lives will intersect in the kind of collectivism you've only read about. Hope will swell big in your heart, and you will be hungry for more because you have been starved. In those moments you learn how much we can change the world. In those moments you taste what collectivism really means and you realize how much we can change the world when we move together.

NOW, LET'S TALK about how to leverage those relationships to create real, lasting safety and disrupt harmful behaviors within your own community. Start by thinking about the people and groups you already know who can help you create more safety around you.

Ask yourself:

▸ **Who makes you feel safe and supported?** Think about the people who make you feel grounded, friends who listen, neighbors who check in, family members who show up. These are the people you can turn to first. Reach out to them not with all the answers, but with your intention: to imagine and build more safety together. Let them know why this matters to you. Ask them what safety means to them.

▸ **Who has skills, resources, or lived experience that could contribute?** Maybe someone in your circle is a teacher, a parent, a trauma-informed healer, or a survivor who has navigated systems firsthand. Others might be great at logistics, cooking, design, or conflict resolution. Don't just look for "leaders"; look for people with insight, capacity, and care. Everyone has something to offer.

▸ **Who can help you reach others?** Identify the connectors, the people who know a lot of folks, are trusted by many, or hold influence in your community. These might be youth leaders, faith leaders, artists, or even someone who runs the local corner store. Their support can help bring others in and legitimize your efforts.

▸ **Where are people already coming together in ways that feel safe and affirming?** Look to the spaces where you already feel connected. That could be a mosque, a school, a local mutual aid group, a book club, or even your own living room. These familiar places can become gathering points for conversations, workshops, or strategy sessions. You don't have to build a new structure; you can repurpose the spaces where community already exists.

▸ **What groups or individuals are already doing safety work in your area?** There may be grassroots organizations, youth programs, domestic violence advocates, or cultural institutions nearby that are already creating safety in powerful ways. Reach out to them. Learn what they're doing. Offer to collaborate or support. Building a movement doesn't have to mean starting from zero; it can mean deepening and connecting what already is.

▸ **How do you invite others in without assuming or imposing?** Approach your people with clarity and care. Share what you're trying to build and why it matters to you. Ask them what safety means in their own lives, and what they've seen work or fail. This isn't about recruiting, it's about co-creating. Real organizing honors where people are coming from and invites them to build something together.

CHANGING SYSTEMS OF VIOLENCE REQUIRES JOY

THIS LAST PART was the hardest thing for me to grasp when I first got into this work because my activism was driven by anger, fear, and pain. The attack I experienced was rooted in hate, and for a long time I responded to that hate with my own insecurity and anxiety. I was fueled by a sense of injustice and the desire to protect myself and others. I mean, how could I not be? How could we all not be so angry? There's so much pain and suffering in our world and in our history, so much violence against us. Let me say: Your anger, sadness, and trauma are so valid. And, honestly, it's been especially hard to find joy lately. There's a lot going on to be angry about.

In 2013 Emory University researchers conducted an experiment that helped us understand the depths of trauma for the first time. They trained a group of mice to fear the smell of cherry blossoms by shocking them every time they introduced the scent. Over time the mice associated the smell of cherry blossoms with fear and pain, even when they weren't shocked. Then the mice had babies and their baby mice also were terrified by the cherry blossom scent even though they had never experienced the scientific experiment themselves. It took four generations for the fear of cherry blossoms to begin to erode, unless intentional healing interventions were introduced.

I first heard this story not from a science journal but from a Palestinian artist. We were gathered before her performance at an Eid dinner I was attending, after two brutal years of a mainstream witnessing of the mass slaughter of Palestinian people, and she shared this story with us. She wasn't just talking about mice. She was talking about herself. She was talking about us. About how grief, terror, and heartbreak live inside us long after the violence. About how even if we survive, the wounds we carry are passed on unless we are deliberate about our healing.

Now think about the world we live in, a world that is constantly inflicting violence on us. Our joy and healing must be deliberate, especially in the spaces where we want to plant the seeds of change. Here's the thing: When we organize from grief alone, when we build only from anger, pain, and loss, we risk building a future that carries those same wounds forward. Anger can keep you going for a while, but it doesn't sustain you in the long run. When we find space to organize with joy, from care, from imagination, from real human connection, we start to interrupt that cycle. We create new imprints: ones rooted in safety, belonging, abundance, and love. Coming back to joy isn't about ignoring the violence around us. It's about choosing, deliberately, to create the kind of emotional inheritance we want to leave behind. When we build safety, we aren't just fighting for survival. We are fighting to plant joy so deep in our communities that it becomes part of who we are, something our future children and grandchildren can inherit without fear. That's why we must start right where we are, with the people we know, and create joy.

Instead of your north star being the harm, what is your vision for the future beyond that harm? If you are against gender-based violence, what are you for? What is the love that will keep you in this work, year after year after year?

Personally, what keeps me in the work, what keeps me from throwing my hands up into the air and just giving up, is my deep love for my community here in Queens. I just want us all to be safe. We Egyptians tell ourselves that we are funny. I believe this to be a fact, but don't ask me for empirical evidence. We say that because of all of our shared hardships, the only way we learned to cope is through humor. It is truly an insult in Egyptian culture if someone is not lighthearted, funny, and joyous; we say "their blood is heavy"—basically, that they did not pass the vibe check. It's the worst thing you can be.

Luckily, I have found so much joy with my immigrant community of women I built with along the way. Malikah isn't just about teaching self-defense techniques. It's pretty common to find a party breakout in the basement of our center.

In spring 2024, I took a bus full of aunties from my neighborhood to the state capitol in Albany to rally for the passage of a bill that would require demographic data that contained information about ancestry to include separate categories for individual Middle Eastern and North African groups. What was intended as a focused, serious advocacy trip about the erasure of our community, domestic violence, the health-care crisis, and gentrification quickly evolved into a lit party bus, thanks to the spirit and joy of my elders. As soon as we boarded the bus, the energy was electric. The chatter soon turned into belly dancing breaks, music blasted through the speakers, and laughter poured from the windows. We also shared powerful stories of erasure, stories of the ways our communities have been overlooked and forgotten by data systems and political structures. But when we think back to the trip now, everyone in our coalition remembers most the energy that was created in that space: pure joy. We showed that, in fighting for justice, we can still find joy, even in the most serious of spaces. In moments of hardship, we have to laugh, dance, and sing to keep going.

The dancing, the singing, and the laughter weren't a dis-traction from the work. They *were* the work. And, of course, the bill passed.

Our goal can't just be about survival; it has to be about us thriving. Those moments of joy, of laughter, of singing songs together weren't frivolous. They were acts of rebellion in a world that constantly tries to make us feel small, pow-erless, and isolated. When we gather to celebrate, when we create joy in the face of suffering, we are defying the forces that want to break us. Audre Lorde's quote is often used to capture this: "Caring for myself is not self-indulgence, it is self-preservation, and that is an act of political warfare." One hundred percent.

MARCH 2020 WAS one of the hardest times of my life. There was a global pandemic, and I would lie awake in bed listening to the nonstop sirens in the street. Then I would tiptoe close enough to my mother's room to watch her as she battled COVID, but far enough away to keep from getting infected. For days, I would check in on her breathing this way. If the comforter tightly wrapped around her body moved up and down, she was alive. There were close calls, of course. I would shout her name into the depths of darkness when I would think she wasn't moving, only to hear a muffled response from underneath layers of fabric: *"Ana kowayisa*, I'm okay," she would say to me. She had caught COVID just as New York City was shutting down, and we held on at home as long as we could, afraid of what might happen if we sought help from overwhelmed hospitals.

The whole time I was watching her so closely, I was also watching my city. My two loves were breaking my heart. Lines wrapped around our local hospitals; isolation was impossible in homes that sheltered multigenerational families in one bedroom; and you can't really work from home if you're a cab driver or street vendor, can you? On my block we tried to organize to do our best to survive. Meals, personal protective equipment, and bags of groceries were distributed. We held fundraisers for local families and local businesses. And there were lots of angry tweets and phone calls to elected officials who seemed to be in a different world. Government help was too slow, too bureaucratic, or nonexistent.

At the time, the only things holding New York City together were the love, joy, and mutual aid networks that organically came together as a result of failed policy and deeply rooted relationships. From friends to fellow organizers, I saw every neighborhood stitch together networks of support, turn empty warehouses into food storage units, drag old refrigerators into community pantries, and raise thousands of dollars to support each other, block by block.

In those moments, care and joy were the difference between charity and mutual aid. It shifted us from mere service to building authentic relationships, creating stronger communities. It sustained our ability to show up and fight to create safety day after day after day. And this isn't just a Queens story. This is the story of people who are creating safety through joy around the entire world.

Joy in organizing doesn't always come from big wins (because sometimes those take years or don't come at all).

Instead, it comes from the small, everyday moments you build. Like Colombian victims of armed conflict living in Catalonia and helping each other to heal through cooking familiar foods and making collective art. It's my Filipina neighbor in Queens, who for thirty years has run a dance and movement organization focused on preserving and retelling her country's colonial history through festivals and performance. Or in the way the civil rights movement in the United States wove song, spirituals, and friendship into the fight against segregation. It's laughing with an elder at a community meeting over a story from their childhood. It's seeing the way someone's whole face lights up after they throw their first punch in a self-defense class. It's sitting together late into the night, exhausted but side by side, holding on to the certainty that you're not alone in the fight. This joy is not frivolous. It is not an escape from struggle or a substitute for organizing. It is the practice that makes this work livable. It keeps people connected to one another. It allows movements to survive long enough to win.

Joy is not abstract; it can begin with you. This guide is an invitation to notice where ease, laughter, and meaning already exist in your life.

✪ RECONNECT WITH YOUR OWN JOY

BEGIN BY REMEMBERING what joy feels like — not the performance of happiness, but the moments of real calm or wonder that have grounded you. Ask yourself:

- ▸ When was the last time I felt genuinely at peace, free, or connected?
- ▸ What was I doing? Who was with me? What was the environment like?
- ▸ How did it feel in my body? Was there warmth, lightness, stillness?

Start to name these moments, whether they're big milestones or brief, quiet flashes in an ordinary day. They're clues to what sustains you.

✪ LOOK TO YOUR COMMUNITY'S JOY

YOU ARE NOT alone in your need for joy. Communities, especially those that have survived systemic harm, have always carved out moments of celebration, even in hardship. Reflect on:

- ▸ What brings joy and connection to my people?
- ▸ What traditions, prayers, holidays, meals, music,

or gatherings create joy in my cultural or spiritual
community?

► How have my elders or ancestors created celebration
in the midst of struggle?

These collective expressions of joy aren't just nostalgia; they are blueprints. They show us how to make room for beauty and meaning, even when the world feels heavy.

✪ CREATE YOUR OWN JOYFUL PRACTICES

JOY DOESN'T HAVE to be spontaneous. It can be a practice, something you commit to and nurture over time. Think of one to four small actions you can build into your routine that make space for happiness, calm, or pleasure. These could be:

► Starting your day with a specific *du'a*, stretch,
or breath
► Taking a walk without your phone and noticing the
world around you
► Listening to music from your childhood
► Dancing in your kitchen
► Calling a friend who makes you laugh
► Cooking something you love

To create safety, you don't have to wait until you feel like you have figured it all out. You already carry what you need: your experiences, your relationships, your instincts. You don't need grand plans, fancy resources, or a perfect strategy. Anyone can create safety. And trust me — we're going to need everyone.

The Fight for Safety Is Bigger Than a Fist

LIKE MANY THINGS in my life, this book was born out of a fight. A deeply personal, deeply relational, deeply political fight against gender-based violence, in our homes, in our streets, in our schools, in our workplaces, online and offline, all over the world. It's a fight I've seen up close. A fight I've watched far too many people carry in silence. And as we've explored together, this violence doesn't just harm individuals. It fractures our communities, corrodes trust, and destabilizes us. Gender-based violence thrives on silence and shame, and in systems that turn their backs.

Even though this is an issue that often is shoved behind closed doors, it's not a secret. It's right here. It shows in the people turned away from shelters. It's clear when survivors are doubted, blamed, and criminalized. When marginalized people are disproportionately harmed and silenced. If it's not happening to you, it's happening to someone you love. And still we're told to keep it quiet. We don't have time for quiet. In New York City, fear is in the air, on the trains, in the streets, on the news. Just 37 percent of New Yorkers say they feel safe in their neighborhoods. Nearly 80 percent don't feel safe riding the subway at night. Instead of addressing the root causes, our elected leaders feed us fear of each other. Fear of immigrants. Fear of poor people. Fear wrapped in overpolicing, armed with batons. And this isn't just a New York story.

It makes sense that some of us are just trying to get by. To keep our heads down, hustle, escape if we can. Stay in our lane and just survive. There's no shame in surviving. But let's not confuse survival with liberation. Not when fascism is rising. Not when they are counting on our disconnection to win.

Our healing, our survival, our safety — that has always been collective. Real safety isn't militarized. It's built. Slowly. Messily. In kitchens, dojos, and classrooms, in prayer circles and protest chants. It's built where our hands meet hands, foot next to foot, knee next to knee.

I've seen it, and it is so beautiful.

It looks like a survivor in Brooklyn who uses her cane not just to walk but to set boundaries. It looks like a survivor leading a healing circle in their neighborhood. It looks like a survivor in Detroit running a savings group for other mamas who want out of unsafe relationships. It looks like teens in Jackson Heights, Queens, teaching self-defense moves to their younger siblings. It looks like someone organizing a block meeting after a neighbor is assaulted. It's building a life we don't have to run from. Now you know what it could look like too.

That's what I've tried to offer here. Not just techniques, but a self-defense framework and a foundation for how we can build a safer world together, because safety is a human right. Everyone should feel safe, no matter who they are or what they look like. It feels more urgent and more important than ever.

Physical self-defense is one important pillar. It reminds our body how to respond when our brain is frozen. It's not about living in fear; it's about moving through the world with readiness. Practicing so deeply that it becomes muscle memory. You learn what your body can do, and you trust it.

Healing as self-defense is another pillar. Because trauma doesn't stay still. It moves through generations. But through being in community with people who see you, through movement, through journaling, through storytelling, through prayer, we can heal together. We need those spaces where we can process, cry, scream, breathe. Where we can say, "That happened to me," and be believed, without question. Where we can ask for help and actually receive it.

We should also build economic power because safety without resources is naïve in this material world. Financial independence is a tool of resistance. Anyone who tells you otherwise likely hasn't been broke before. Financial stability and material well-being allow us to walk away from what harms us. That's why we build community savings circles. We spend our money with our people. Every dollar's value is in how we earn it and how we spend it.

And, of course, we have to organize our communities to change policy and systems, starting with whom we know, what we know, and joy, because things don't change on their own. We organize because we shouldn't need to learn self-defense to begin with, we shouldn't have to rely on markets for housing, we shouldn't need to heal from trauma. Trauma, violence, and insecure financial circumstances shouldn't exist, and we can get closer to a world where that is true if we have better structures and policies that economically dignify our communities, create safety, and don't perpetuate trauma.

Lots of my friends and family see what I do and question whether the work is worth it. They remind me how hard it is. They see the endless nights of holding survivors in my arms, heart, and soul. But through this work I have gained a level of hope that has allowed bits and parts of my soul to be free. I've watched women come into a class uncertain, unsure they even belong in the room, and leave with new language, new tools, new people on speed dial. I've seen survivors lead. Teens plan. Aunties trade phone numbers and exit plans. To bear witness to this kind of change creates the kind of joy that bursts in your chest. It grows flowers of hope in dry soil.

I HOPE YOU see the end of this book as the beginning of your own vision for a different kind of world. So ask yourself: What's your next step? What's in your safety bag? Who's on your call list? What techniques are you going to practice? Whom are you building with?

This book ostensibly is about the fight, but this book was born out of love. The kind of fierce, steady love that keeps us showing up. Love that teaches, that protects, that makes room for us even when the world does not. It came from kitchen-table conversations with aunties who survived more than they have ever spoken aloud. From community circles where women looked each other in the eye and said, "I've been there too." From the little girls in our workshops who learned how to say no for the first time and meant it. From the late-night calls with a friend deciding if she should leave. From a mother teaching her daughter how to breathe, strike, and speak her truth. I wish you both the fight and love to help build a safer world. You don't have to do everything. But you do have to begin, especially when it feels like the world is unraveling around you. You just have to grab on to the loose threads around you and hold tight. If enough of us do that, together, we'll weave something stronger than the insecurity we've been handed. Something worth living for. A world where we don't have to tell each other to "get home safe."

Acknowledgments

FIRST AND FOREMOST, to my parents. From the very beginning, when no one else believed this vision was possible, you stood by me. You enrolled me in karate even when it meant going against the grain, and in doing so you opened a path for me that I never could have imagined. You have been there at every turn, from distributing food in our neighborhood to picking up the pieces when things grew heavy. Your sacrifices, faith, and unwavering support have been the roots of everything I have built. This book carries your fingerprints.

To my husband, Aziz Ramos, and my new baby, you are my heart and my anchor. You remind me daily of why this work matters. Your love, patience, and inspiration keep me grounded and give me the courage to keep going, even in the hardest moments. You are my greatest joy.

To my sister, Jenna, an extraordinary martial artist who has pushed and challenged me as both an athletic partner and a thought partner. You have made me braver, sharper, and stronger.

To my senseis, Mostafa and Yasser, who first taught me karate. You instilled in me the values of discipline, humility, and resilience, and guided me on the journey to earning my black belt. The lessons you gave me on the mat shaped how I move through the world, as an athlete and as a leader.

To Nada Elshafey, Deena Hadhoud, and Hind Essayegh, women who embody what it means to take a vision and breathe life into it. Nada, through your mutual aid leadership, you have shown me how financial well-being begins in the neighborhood, where neighbors take care of one another. Deena, I trained you when you had no martial arts background, and you carried the Malikah model forward, training so many others with creativity and courage. Hind, with your martial arts expertise and your willingness to test and refine the curriculum beside me, you became a true thought partner. Each of you has expanded Malikah in ways I could never have done alone.

To my dear friends and co-organizers, Fawzia, Sabah, Jaylan, Noor, and Adama. You are my daily teachers and companions in this work. You have carried Malikah with steadiness and vision, holding the helm when the waters got rough. From you I learn, again and again, what collective leadership, trust, and resilience look like.

To Madeline Jones, my editor, for guiding me through the daunting process of writing my first book and for helping me translate ideas I once thought belonged only in classrooms onto these pages. And to Elias Altman, who believed in this vision from the very start and helped me carry it forward.

And finally, to the immigrant working class women in my Queens neighborhood, the aunties who opened their hearts to me, the young girls who came to classes with curiosity and fire, the mothers who showed up even after long days of work, the sisters who reminded me that joy and struggle live side by side. You are the reason this work exists. You showed me that safety is built not only in classrooms or on mats but in hallways, stoops, parks, and living rooms. This book is, above all, a love letter to you.

Notes

Introduction

Almost 53 percent of women in the United States: Lydia Saad, "Personal Safety Fears at Three-Decade High in U.S.," Gallup, November 16, 2023, https://news.gallup.com/poll/544415/personal-safety-fears-three-decade-high.aspx.

Fifty percent of women in the United States feel unsafe: Jeni Klugman and Elena Ortiz, "Half of American Women Feel Unsafe Because They Are Women," EMERGE, University of California San Diego, March 31, 2021, https://emerge.ucsd.edu/half-of-american-women-feel-unsafe-because-they-are-women/.

Eighty-one percent of women report experiencing: "Sexual Assault Statistics," National Sexual Violence Resource Center, accessed September 13, 2025, https://www.nsvrc.org/statistics.

One in three women who've been in a relationship: "One in Three Women Experiences Gender-Based Violence," UN News, November 15, 2024, https://news.un.org/en/story/2024/11/1157046.

One in six women in the United States: "Facts and Statistics: The Scope of the Problem," RAINN, accessed September 13, 2025, https://rainn.org/get-informed/facts-statistics-the-scope-of-the-problem/.

Around the world, every ten minutes: "One Woman or Girl Is Killed Every 10 Minutes by Their Intimate Partner or Family Member," UN Women, November 25, 2024, https://www.unwomen.org/en/news-stories/press-release/2024/11/one-woman-or-girl-is-killed-every-10-minutes-by-their-intimate-partner-or-family-member.

pregnant women are more likely to be murdered: "Homicide Leading
Cause of Death for Pregnant Women in U.S.," Harvard T. H. Chan
School of Public Health, October 21, 2022, https://hsph.harvard.edu
/news/homicide-leading-cause-of-death-for-pregnant-women-in-u-s/.

Yet 75 percent of women murdered by their partners: Jana Kasperkevic,
"Private Violence: Up to 75% of Abused Women Who Are Murdered
Are Killed After They Leave Their Partners," *The Guardian*, October
20, 2014, https://www.theguardian.com/money/us-money-blog/2014
/oct/20/domestic-private-violence-women-men-abuse-hbo-ray-rice.

Women ages eighteen to twenty-four: "Statistics: Victims of Sexual
Violence," RAINN, accessed September 13, 2025, https://rainn.org
/facts-statistics-the-scope-of-the-problem/statistics-victims-of-sexual
-violence/.

In the workplace, women are twice as likely: "Violence and Harassment at Work Has Affected More than One in Five People," International Labour Organization, December 5, 2022, https://www.ilo.org
/resource/news/violence-and-harassment-work-has-affected-more-one
-five-people.

Thirty-eight percent of women: "Online Violence," Amnesty International, accessed September 13, 2025, https://www.amnesty.org/en
/what-we-do/technology/online-violence/.

Twenty-one percent of us carry pepper spray: Carol W. Runyan,
Carri Casteel, Kathryn E. Moracco, and Tamera Coyne-Beasley, "US
Women's Choices of Strategies to Protect Themselves from Violence,"
Injury Prevention 13, no. 4 (August 2007): 270–275, https://pmc.ncbi
.nlm.nih.gov/articles/PMC2598334/.

Almost 90 percent of women in Nepal, India, and Pakistan:
"Violence Against Women in Politics," UN Women, 2014, https://
www.unwomen.org/en/digital-library/publications/2014/6/violence
-against-women-in-politics.

the global economy loses $1.6 trillion annually: Rasmane Ouedraogo
and David Stenzel, "The Heavy Economic Toll of Gender-Based
Violence: Evidence from Sub-Saharan Africa," Working Paper

No. 277, International Monetary Fund, November 19, 2021, https://doi.org/10.5089/9781557754073.001.

"As long as women are using class": bell hooks, *Feminism Is for Everybody: Passionate Politics* (Cambridge, MA: South End Press, 2000), 16.

Mainstream feminist movements rarely fought: Margo Mahan, "The Racial Origins of U.S. Domestic Violence Law" (PhD dissertation, University of California, 2017), https://escholarship.org/uc/item/0zs890k1.

As Lila Abu-Lughod writes: Lila Abu-Lughod, *Do Muslim Women Need Saving?* (Cambridge, MA: Harvard University Press, 2013).

In the twentieth century, Native women were disproportionately: Lisa Ko, "Unwanted Sterilization and Eugenics Programs in the United States," *Independent Lens* (PBS), January 29, 2016, https://www.pbs.org/independentlens/blog/unwanted-sterilization-and-eugenics-programs-in-the-united-states/.

"Feminism in the United States has never emerged": bell hooks, *Feminist Theory: From Margin to Center* (Boston: South End Press, 1984), 1.

Rule #1: Start with Healing

As of 2021, an estimated 86 percent: "Female Genital Mutilation," UNFPA Egypt, accessed September 30, 2025, https://egypt.unfpa.org/en/topics/female-genital-mutilation.

Today the number is closer to 80 percent: "Female Genital Mutilation," UNFPA Egypt, accessed September 30, 2025, https://egypt.unfpa.org/en/topics/female-genital-mutilation.

In fact, in the 1960s an Ohio gynecologist: Sara Johnsdotter, "Projected Cultural Histories of the Cutting of Female Genitalia: A Poor Reflection as in a Mirror," *History and Anthropology* 23, no. 1 (March 2012): 91–114, https://www.diva-portal.org/smash/get/diva2:1401455/FULLTEXT01.pdf.

Bessel Van der Kolk: Bessel A. Van der Kolk, *The Body Keeps the Score: Brain, Mind, and Body in the Healing of Trauma* (New York: Viking, 2014).

After 9/11, hate crimes against Muslims: Ilir Disha, James C. Cavendish, and Ryan D. King, "Historical Events and Spaces of Hate: Hate Crimes Against Arabs and Muslims in Post-9/11 America," *Social Problems* 58, no. 1 (February 2011): 21–46, https://www.albany.edu/news/images /Hate_crimes_study.pdf.

"Feminism is a movement to end sexism": bell hooks, *Feminism Is for Everybody: Passionate Politics* (Cambridge, MA: South End Press, 2000), viii.

As Paulo Freire wrote: Paulo Freire, *Pedagogy of the Oppressed*, 30th anniversary ed., trans. Myra Bergman Ramos (New York: Continuum, 2000).

"white men saving brown women": Gayatri Chakravorty Spivak, "Can the Subaltern Speak?," in *Marxism and the Interpretation of Culture*, ed. Cary Nelson and Lawrence Grossberg, 271–313 (Urbana: University of Illinois Press, 1988).

the work of Frantz Fanon: Frantz Fanon, "Algeria Unveiled," in *A Dying Colonialism*, trans. Haakon Chevalier, 35–67 (New York: Grove Press, 1965).

Studies show that trauma-informed group interventions: Lisa A. Goodman and Deborah Epstein, *Listening to Battered Women: A Survivor-Centered Approach to Advocacy, Mental Health, and Justice* (Washington, DC: American Psychological Association, 2008).

Rule #3: Stay Sharp

Gavin De Becker: Gavin De Becker, *The Gift of Fear: Survival Signals That Protect Us from Violence* (New York: Dell, 1997).

Carol Gilligan: Carol Gilligan, *In a Different Voice: Psychological Theory and Women's Development* (Cambridge, MA: Harvard University Press, 1982).

Research on emotional labor: Arlie Russell Hochschild, *The Managed Heart: Commercialization of Human Feeling*, 20th anniversary ed. (Berkeley: University of California Press, 2003).

Studies show that women's pain: Diane E. Hoffman and Anita J. Tarzian, "The Girl Who Cried Pain: A Bias Against Women in the

Treatment of Pain," *Journal of Law, Medicine and Ethics* 29, no. 1 (Spring 2001): 13–27, https://doi.org/10.1111/j.1748-720X.2001.tb00037.x.

Studies in neuroscience: Simon Baron-Cohen, *The Essential Difference: Men, Women and the Extreme Male Brain* (London: Allen Lane, 2003).

Other studies have consistently shown: Alexander Lausen and Annekathrin Schacht, "Gender Differences in the Recognition of Vocal Emotions," *Frontiers in Psychology* 9 (2018): 882, https://www.frontiersin.org/journals/psychology/articles/10.3389/fpsyg.2018.00882/full.

people who use their phones while walking: Ira E. Hyman, S. Matthew Boss, Breanne M. Wise, and Kira E. McKenzie, "Did You See the Unicycling Clown? Inattentional Blindness While Walking and Talking on a Cell Phone," *Applied Cognitive Psychology* 24, no. 5 (July 2009): 597–607, https://onlinelibrary.wiley.com/doi/10.1002/acp.1638.

Gloria Mark: American Psychological Association. "Why Our Attention Spans Are Shrinking, with Gloria Mark, PhD." *Speaking of Psychology* (podcast) (February 8, 2023), https://www.apa.org/news/podcasts/speaking-of-psychology/attention-spans.

Rule #4: Deescalate with Your Voice and Body

Sources consulted for this chapter:

"The 5Ds of Bystander Intervention," Right to Be, accessed September 13, 2025, https://righttobe.org/guides/bystander-intervention-training/.

Peter Fischer, Joachim I. Krueger, Tobias Greitemeyer, Claudia Vogrincic, Andreas Kastenmüller, Dieter Frey, et al., "The Bystander-Effect: A Meta-Analytic Review on Bystander Intervention in Dangerous and Non-Dangerous Emergencies," *Psychological Bulletin* 137, no. 4 (July 2011): 517–537, https://doi.org/10.1037/a0023304.

Martin Gansberg, "37 Who Saw Murder Didn't Call the Police," *New York Times*, March 27, 1964.

Bibb Latané and John M. Darley, "Group Inhibition of Bystander Intervention in Emergencies," *Journal of Personality and Social Psychology* 10, no. 3 (1968): 215–221, https://psycnet.apa.org/doi/10.1037/h0026570.

Rachel Manning, Mark Levine, and Alan Collins, "The Kitty Genovese Murder and the Social Psychology of Helping: The Parable
of the 38 Witnesses," *American Psychologist* 62, no. 6 (September
2007): 555–562, https://psycnet.apa.org/doi/10.1037/0003-066X.62
.6.555.

Rule #5: Strike Back (Only If You Need To)

In late 2023, the United Nations released: "Femicides in 2023: Global
Estimates of Intimate-Partner / Family Member Femicides," United
Nations Women and United Nations Office on Drugs and Crime,
November 25, 2024, https://www.unwomen.org/sites/default
/files/2024-11/femicides-in-2023-global-estimates-of-intimate-partner
-family-member-femicides-en.pdf.

On average, 140 women and girls: Edith M. Lederer, "An Average of
140 Women and Girls Were Killed by a Partner or Relative per Day
in 2023, the UN Says," Associated Press, November 25, 2024, https://
apnews.com/article/un-killing-women-girls-partners-family-global
-c2f26290b8158e1d97b1b16ef76e85a8.

Other sources consulted for this chapter:

Lizette Alvarez, "Florida Woman Sentenced to 20 Years in Prison for
Firing a Gun," *New York Times*, May 11, 2012, https://www.nytimes
.com/2012/05/12/us/marissa-alexander-of-florida-sentenced-to-20
-years-for-firing-gun.htm.

Jeannine Monnier, "Women Face Harsher Punishments When It
Comes to Self-Defense Laws," *Monitor on Psychology*, April–May 2025,
https://www.apa.org/monitor/2025/04-05/sentencing-women
-abuse-survivors.

Debbie Mukamal, Andrea N. Cimino, Blyss Cleveland, Emma Dougherty,
Jacqueline Lewittes, and Becca Zimmerman, "Fatal Peril: Unheard
Stories from the IPV-to-Prison Pipeline," rev. ed., Stanford Criminal
Justice Center, 2024, https://law.stanford.edu/wp-content
/uploads/2024/08/Fatal-Peril-Final.pdf.

"Self-Defense and 'Stand Your Ground,'" National Conference of State Legislatures, updated March 1, 2023, https://www.ncsl.org/civil-and -criminal-justice/self-defense-and-stand-your-ground.

Rachel Louise Snyder, "Who Gets to Kill in Self-Defense?," *New York Times*, September 4, 2024, https://www.nytimes.com/interactive /2024/09/04/opinion/women-kill-self-defense.html.

Rule #6: Expect the Unexpected

Sources consulted for this chapter:

Ashley Southall, "Man Pushes Woman into Path of Subway Train in Times Square," *New York Times*, January 16, 2022, https://www .nytimes.com/2022/01/16/nyregion/michelle-go-man-pushes-woman -subway.html.

Rule #7: Secure the Bag, Secure Your Safety

According to a 2021 study: "Power: Supporting Local Businesses," First United Bank, October 29, 2025, https://www.firstunitedbank.com /spendlifewisely/power-supporting-local-businesses.

In fact, 59 percent of Americans: Cynthia Griffith, "59% of Americans Are Just One Paycheck Away from Homelessness," Invisible People, accessed September 13, 2025, https://invisiblepeople.tv/59-of -americans-are-just-one-paycheck-away-from-homelessness/.

New York City providers report that housing and shelter: National Network to End Domestic Violence, "19th Annual Domestic Violence Counts Report," 2025, NNEDV.org/DVCounts.

Rule #8: Build a Safer World Together

Between 2019 and 2023, the national average: "National Summary of Homeless System Performance Measures, 2019–2023," US Department of Housing and Urban Development, revised June 11, 2024, https:// files.hudexchange.info/resources/documents/National-Summary-of -Homeless-System-Performance.pdf.

Across the United States, 57 percent: Ellie Kurrus, "DV Is the Leading Cause of Homelessness Among Women," All Against Abuse, accessed September 14, 2025, https://allagainstabuse.org/homelessness-among -women.

as of 2025 the average cost for full-time: Erik Bascome, "Childcare Costs 2025: Which States Are Most Expensive for Parents?," CCC New York, July 14, 2025, https://cccnewyork.org/press-and-media/childcare -costs-2025-which-states-are-most-expensive-for-parents/.

Even for those whose asylum applications: "Asylum in the United States," fact sheet, American Immigration Council, May 9, 2025, https://www.americanimmigrationcouncil.org/fact-sheet/asylum -united-states/.

Za'atari, a refugee camp in Jordan: "Life in Za'atari, the Largest Syrian Refugee Camp in the World," Oxfam International, accessed September 21, 2025, https://www.oxfam.org/en/life-zaatari-largest-syrian -refugee-camp-world.

Forty-one percent of the women and girls: "Woman Alone: The Fight for Survival by Syria's Refugee Women," UN High Commissioner for Refugees, 2014, https://www.unhcr.org/sites/default/files/legacy -pdf/53bb8d006.pdf.

Fifty percent of the survivors: "Sexual and Gender-Based Violence: Syrian Refugees in Jordan," Sexual and Gender-Based Violence Sub-Working Group Jordan, March 2014.

Sofia, like 26.4 percent of all women in US colleges: "Statistics: Campus Sexual Violence," RAINN, accessed September 14, 2025, https://rainn .org/facts-statistics-the-scope-of-the-problem/statistics-campus-sexual -violence/.

Six out of ten victims of rape and sexual assault: "Victims and the Individuals Who Commit Sexual Violence," National Institute of Justice, October 26, 2010, https://nij.ojp.gov/topics/articles/victims-and -individuals-who-commit-sexual-violence.

Unsurprising, since more than 90 percent: "Going to College: What Families Need to Know About Sexual Assault and Safety on Campus," National Sexual Violence Resource Center, June 2016, https://www

.nsvrc.org/sites/default/files/2016-06/publications_nsvrc_tip-sheet _going-to-college-what-families-need-know-sexual-assault-safety -campus.pdf.

Cuomo was about to relaunch his entry into politics: Nick Reisman, "DOJ Says Andrew Cuomo Sexually Harassed 13 Women," *Politico*, January 26, 2024, https://www.politico.com/news/2024/01/26 /cuomo-sexual-harassment-doj-00138140.

a report released by the New York State attorney general: Office of the Attorney General, State of New York, "Report of Investigation into Allegations of Sexual Harassment by Governor Andrew M. Cuomo," August 3, 2021, https://ag.ny.gov/sites/default/files/2021.08.03_nyag _investigative_report.pdf.

To borrow from the Argentinian fourth-wave: Jaclyn Diaz, "How #NiUnaMenos Grew from the Streets of Argentina into a Regional Women's Movement," NPR, October 15, 2021, https://www.npr .org/2021/10/15/1043908435/how-niunamenos-grew-from-the-streets -of-argentina-into-a-regional-womens-movement.

Liberia, much like Sudan: Selina Gallo-Cruz and Renée Remsberg, "Peacebuilding, Liberian Women, and the Invisible Hand of Conflict in the Postwar Era," *Journal of Social Encounters* 5, no. 2 (2021): article 8, https://digitalcommons.csbsju.edu/cgi/viewcontent.cgi? article=1094&context=social_encounters.

That day Leymah reminded us that 70 percent: Katelyn M. Sileo, Trace S. Kershaw, Shantesica Gilliam, Erica Taylor, Apoorva Kommajosula, and Tamora A. Callands, "Trauma Exposure and Intimate Partner Violence Among Young Pregnant Women in Liberia," *Journal of Interpersonal Violence* 36, nos. 21–22 (2019): 10101–10127, https://pmc.ncbi .nlm.nih.gov/articles/PMC7778451/.

relational organizing expert Marshall Ganz: "Leading Change: Leadership, Organization, and Social Movements," in *Handbook of Leadership Theory and Practice: A Harvard Business School Centennial Colloquium*, edited by Nitin Nohria and Rakesh Khurana (Boston: Harvard Business Publishing, 2010), 527–568.

On June 17, Nabra Hassanen: "Nabra Hassanen: Virginia Man Admits Murder of Teenage Girl," BBC News, November 28, 2018, https://www.bbc.com/news/world-us-canada-46376292.

In 2013 Emory University researchers: "Mice Can Inherit Learned Sensitivity to a Smell," Emory University News Center, December 2, 2013, https://news.emory.edu/stories/2013/12/smell_epigenetics_ressler/.

"Caring for myself is not self-indulgence": Audre Lorde, *A Burst of Light: And Other Essays* (Ithaca, NY: Firebrand Books, 1988), 131.

Conclusion: The Fight for Safety Is Bigger Than a Fist

Just 37 percent of New Yorkers: Elijah Westbrook and Marcia Kramer, "New Yorkers Are Not Satisfied with Quality of Life in NYC, Survey Finds," CBS New York, June 4, 2025, https://www.cbsnews.com/newyork/news/new-yorkers-say-quality-of-life-safety-have-declined-in-recent-years-according-to-new-survey/.

Nearly 80 percent don't feel safe: Andrés Correa, "78% teme viajar de noche en el Metro de Nueva York: Encuesta arroja alta infelicidad en la ciudad," *El Diario*, March 20, 2024, https://eldiariony.com/2024/03/20/78-teme-viajar-de-noche-en-el-metro-de-nueva-york-encuesta-arroja-alta-infelicidad-en-la-ciudad/.

About the Author

Rana Abdelhamid, aka the "Mayor of Queens," is a daughter of Egyptian immigrants and was born and raised in Queens. She's a black belt in karate; a creative, lifelong organizer; a new mom; and the 2025 David Prize winner. Abdelhamid is the founder of Malikah, a grassroots organization with a storefront in Astoria, which offers self-defense and bystander training and trauma-informed healing. Through Malikah, she and her team have trained over 20,000 people in self-defense across more than thirty cities worldwide.

Abdelhamid's work centers on survivors of gender- and hate-based violence and people in marginalized communities across the city, but her vision of safety goes far beyond defense. Her Astoria space also operates as a food pantry and a safe mailing address for unhoused neighbors. She also founded the Queens Organizing Alliance, which brings people together through regular meetups to build collective power, friendship, and solidarity across the borough, and she led the successful campaign for New York's first MENA data disaggregation law, ensuring Middle Eastern and North

African communities are counted in New York. In 2025, she co-curated an exhibition at MoMA PS1 that celebrated the stories and contributions of North African New Yorkers, bringing visibility and cultural depth to a community often overlooked in mainstream narratives.

Her storytelling platform, Hijabis of New York, lifts up the voices of Muslim women across the five boroughs, and each year she gathers hundreds of Muslim women at the National Muslim Women's Summit. Her work has been recognized by the Forbes 30 Under 30 list, a NYC Council Proclamation, and the Truman Scholarship, and she holds a master's degree in public policy from Harvard Kennedy School. Abdelhamid is building more spaces across New York City where care, safety, and connection are not the exception but the norm, all while embracing the joys and challenges of new motherhood.

RAISING READERS
Books Build Bright Futures

Thank you for reading this book and for being a reader of books in general. We are so grateful to share being part of a community of readers with you, and we hope you will join us in passing our love of books on to the next generation of readers.

Did you know that reading for enjoyment is the single biggest predictor of a child's future happiness and success?

More than family circumstances, parents' educational background, or income, reading impacts a child's future academic performance, emotional well-being, communication skills, economic security, ambition, and happiness.

Studies show that kids reading for enjoyment in the US is in rapid decline:

- In 2012, 53% of 9-year-olds read almost every day. Just 10 years later, in 2022, the number had fallen to 39%.
- In 2012, 27% of 13-year-olds read for fun daily. By 2023, that number was just 14%.

Together, we can commit to **Raising Readers** and change this trend. How?

- Read to children in your life daily.
- Model reading as a fun activity.
- Reduce screen time.
- Start a family, school, or community book club.
- Visit bookstores and libraries regularly.
- Listen to audiobooks.
- Read the book before you see the movie.
- Encourage your child to read aloud to a pet or stuffed animal.
- Give books as gifts.
- Donate books to families and communities in need.

BOB1217

Books build bright futures, and **Raising Readers** is our shared responsibility.

For more information, visit **JoinRaisingReaders.com**

Sources: National Endowment for the Arts, National Assessment of Educational Progress, WorldBookDay.com, Nielsen BookData's 2023 "Understanding the Children's Book Consumer"